复旦卓越·21世纪管理学系列

管理沟通
原理与实践(双语)

张琰 主编

MANAGEMENT COMMUNICATION:
PRINCIPLES AND PRACTICES

复旦大学出版社

内 容 提 要

　　管理沟通是管理学科中的核心课程之一，是研究提高管理行为有效性的一门学科。旨在通过管理沟通的理念、策略与技能的学习，帮助学生了解现代企业管理情境中的沟通问题，全面提高学生的沟通技能和水平，培养学生在群体活动和团队管理中的领导力，促使学生在团队合作中提高成员之间的沟通与合作效率。

　　本书分三大部分，分别从理论、应用、实务三个方面培养学生的理论与实践能力。为了满足双语教学的需要，本书对英文内容进行概要翻译，以增进读者对知识点的理解，有助于学生深度理解理论内容，同时提高英文阅读水平。

前　　言

　　有效沟通是通向成功之路的基石。

　　沟通是人与人之间、人与群体之间信息的传递、作用与反馈的过程。在日常人际交往中，在企业组织中，有效沟通是解决问题的最佳途径。特别是当今世界面临"百年未有之大变局"，更需要各方之间通过沟通交流增进理解、弥合分歧、促进合作。

　　本书旨在通过管理沟通的理念、策略与技能的学习，帮助读者了解现代企业管理情境中的沟通问题，全面提高沟通技能和水平，培养群体活动和团队管理中的领导力，促进沟通与合作效率。

　　本书将基础理论、沟通实践与技能训练有机整合，内容设置上分为三大篇。第一篇介绍了有效沟通原理，包括第1～8章，对管理沟通的七大要素进行了细致分析，并引入"全景分析框架"，帮助读者全面剖析沟通问题。第二篇是管理沟通实践，包括第9～11章，介绍了团队沟通、危机沟通、跨文化沟通的策略与技巧，帮助读者提高沟通实践效果。第三篇是有效沟通技能，包括第12～14章，介绍了有效沟通技能，提供了公众演讲、个人简历、商务邮件等几种常见沟通形式的实务训练。此外，本书在每章内容之后设置了案例分析或延伸阅读栏目，选择中国现实社会中曾经发生的案例作为阅读素材，帮助读者更好地融入情境，促进对有效沟通的理解和反思。

　　为了满足双语教学的需要，本书对英文内容进行概要翻译，以增进读者对知识点的理解。施雰涵、顾依秋、黄卓行等参与了本书部分章节的编写，施雰涵对全书英文翻译进行了总体润色。

　　囿于时间和能力限制，本书仍有诸多局限和不足，望读者海涵并提出宝贵建议！

张　琰

2020年9月

Content
目 录

Section 1　Principles on Effective Communication
第1篇　有效沟通原理

Chapter 1　Foundation of Communication
第1章　沟通基础原理　/3

 1.1　What Is Communication?
 一、什么是沟通　/3
 1.2　Research Developments on Management Communication
 二、管理沟通的研究进展　/4
 1.3　Elements of Communication
 三、沟通要素　/11
 1.4　Why Management Communication Is Important
 四、管理沟通的重要性　/13
 【Conclusion】本章小结　/14
 【Study Questions】课后问题　/15

Chapter 2　Source: How to be a Successful Communicator
第2章　如何做一个成功的沟通者　/16

 2.1　Goodwill
 一、良好意愿　/16
 2.2　You-Attitude
 二、换位思考　/17

2.3　Credibility

三、增加可信度　/20

【Conclusion】本章小结　/24

【Reading Material】Johari Window 约哈里窗户　/25

【Case Study】案例讨论　/26

【Study Questions】课后问题　/27

Chapter 3　Setting Goals
第3章　设定沟通目标　/28

3.1　Setting SMART Goals

一、设定目标　/28

3.2　Sorting Goals

二、目标的分类　/33

3.3　Context Testing by Defining Urgency and Importance

三、基于紧迫性和重要性进行情境分析　/34

【Conclusion】本章小结　/37

【Case Study】案例讨论　/37

【Study Questions】课后问题　/39

Chapter 4　Audience Analysis
第4章　听众分析　/40

4.1　The Framework of Audience Analysis

一、听众分析框架　/40

4.2　Define Your Audience

二、明确沟通对象　/41

4.3　Relationship Analysis

三、听众关系分析　/44

4.4　Assess Audience Attitudes

四、评估听众态度　/45

4.5　Ascertain Audience Knowledge

　　五、确定听众知识背景　/47

4.6　Arouse Audience Interests

　　六、激发听众兴趣　/47

【Conclusion】本章小结　/49

【Case Study】案例讨论　/50

【Study Questions】课后问题　/53

Chapter 5　The Message: Designing Contents and Structures
第5章　沟通的信息：设计内容与结构　/54

5.1　Clarifying Point of View

　　一、明确沟通观点　/54

5.2　Designing Message

　　二、设计沟通信息　/56

5.3　Shaping Your Argument

　　三、形成论点　/57

【Conclusion】本章小结　/62

【Case Study】案例讨论　/63

【Study Questions】课后问题　/64

Chapter 6　Communication Channels
第6章　沟通渠道　/65

6.1　Communication Channel Types

　　一、沟通渠道类型　/65

6.2　Considerations and Skills on Media Choices

　　二、媒体选择技巧　/68

【Conclusion】本章小结　/72

【Case Study】案例讨论　/72

【Study Questions】课后问题　/74

Chapter 7   Feedbacks
第7章　反馈　/75

7.1   Feedback Essentials
一、有效反馈的特征　/75

7.2   Giving Effective Feedbacks
二、提出有效反馈　/79

7.3   Receiving Feedbacks
三、接收反馈　/83

【Conclusion】本章小结　/87

【Study Questions】课后问题　/87

Chapter 8   Put It Together: Panoramic Analysis on Communication Strategy
第8章　管理沟通策略之全景分析　/88

8.1   Framework on Panoramic Analysis
一、管理沟通全景分析　/88

8.2   Panoramic Analysis on Communication Strategies
二、沟通全景分析的五大策略　/92

【Conclusion】本章小结　/108

【Case Study】案例讨论　/108

【Study Questions】课后问题　/110

Section 2   Practices on Management Communication
第2篇　管理沟通实践

Chapter 9   Team Communication
第9章　团队沟通　/113

9.1   What Is Team Communication
一、什么是团队沟通　/113

9.2   Team Conflict and Effective Communication
二、团队冲突与有效沟通　/116

9.3　Skills on Effective Team Communication

　　三、有效团队沟通的技巧　/118

【Conclusion】本章小结　/120

【Case Study】案例讨论　/121

【Study Questions】课后问题　/122

Chapter 10　Crisis Communication
第10章　危机沟通　/123

10.1　Definition and Classification of Crisis

　　一、危机的定义与分类　/123

10.2　Crisis Communication Targets

　　二、危机沟通对象　/126

10.3　Crisis Communication Strategies

　　三、危机沟通策略　/129

【Conclusion】本章小结　/142

【Case Study】案例讨论　/142

【Study Questions】课后问题　/144

Chapter 11　Cross-Cultural Communication
第11章　跨文化沟通　/145

11.1　The Dimensions of Culture

　　一、文化维度理论　/145

11.2　Skills and Techniques of Cross-Cultural Communication

　　二、跨文化沟通技巧　/152

11.3　Strategies of Cross-Cultural Communication

　　三、跨文化管理策略　/156

【Conclusion】本章小结　/158

【Case Study】案例讨论　/158

【Study Questions】课后问题　/159

Section 3   Effective Communication Skills
第3篇   有效沟通技能

Chapter 12   Effective Speaking
第12章   有效演讲   /163

12.1   Definition and Types of Presentation

一、演讲的定义与类型   /163

12.2   Structure of Presentation

二、演讲的结构   /167

12.3   Skills and Techniques

三、演讲技巧   /170

【Conclusion】本章小结   /176

【Exercises】实务练习   /177

【Study Questions】课后问题   /179

Chapter 13   Resume and Job Application Letter
第13章   撰写简历   /180

13.1   The Basics of Resume

一、求职简历基础   /180

13.2   Preparation for a Resume

二、求职简历的前期准备   /184

13.3   Write A Resume

三、简历撰写   /187

13.4   Job Application Letter

四、求职信   /190

【Conclusion】本章小结   /194

【Exercises】实务练习   /194

【Study Questions】课后问题   /198

Chapter 14　Business Writing
第14章　商务写作　/199

14.1　The General Process of Business Writing

一、商务写作的基本流程　/199

14.2　Proposals and Reports

二、商业计划书和报告　/206

14.3　How to Write a Business Email

三、商务电子邮件写作　/209

【Conclusion】本章小结　/215

【Exercises】实务练习　/215

【Study Questions】课后问题　/218

References

参考文献　/219

Section 1: Principles on Effective Communication

第 1 篇　有效沟通原理

Chapter 1   Foundation of Communication
第 1 章   沟通基础原理

> *The art of communication is the language of leadership.*
> ——James Humes

Communication not only affects interpersonal relationships, but also has an important impact on the quality of daily work, project completion and resource allocation in the company. In fact, there is more to communication than just talk and gesture. Listening, giving and receiving feedbacks are as much integral to communication as words — verbal, written or gestured. And the knowledge combines management, economics, psychology and any other social science, which puts forward a high request to the managers.

In this chapter, you will:
- know the research developments on managerial communication;
- understand the essentials of management communication.

1.1 What Is Communication?

Communication is of great importance for managers in terms of improving corporate performance. *The Cambridge Dictionary* defines

沟通不仅影响人际关系，同样对公司的日常工作、项目达成、资源分配有重要影响。沟通包含了表达、倾听、反馈的整合过程，是一个包含管理、经济、心理以及其他社会科学的复杂学科。管理者的沟通水平对提高管理者绩效具有重要意义。

这一章将阐述沟通在管理研究的领域的进展以及形成有效沟通的基本要素。

一、什么是沟通

沟通被定义为"通过电话、电脑、广播等各种媒介在人群和场所中使用多种方

the word "communication" as "various methods of sending information between people and places, especially phones, computers, radio, etc." From the definition three features of communication could be summarized as: ① The content of communication is information. ② Communication is a two-way process rather than a one-way process. ③ It requires medium in order to communicate effectively.

Kitty. O. Locker in *Business and Administrative Communication* (6th Ed.) proposed five purposes of communication, including coordination, knowledge sharing, information gathering, relationship building and conflict resolving.

法传递信息"。

沟通有五种目的：协调、分享知识、信息收集、构建关系以及解决冲突。

1.2 Research Developments on Management Communication

Management communication could be traced back to 5000BC, when Sumerians in ancient Mesopotamia invented a kind of bookkeeping to record the daily business. Researchers contributed to the subject from different approaches.

1. Scientific Management

Managers in the early 1900s had very few external resources to draw upon to guide and develop their management practice. But thanks to Henri Fayol (1841-1925), one of the early theorists on management, managers began to get the tools they needed to lead and manage more effectively. Fayol, memorized for building the foundations of modern management theory, proposed comprehensive statements of a general theory on management.

二、管理沟通的研究进展

最早的管理沟通可以追溯到公元前5000年，苏美尔人通过簿记来记录日常事务。

1. 科学管理

作为古典管理理论的代表人物，法约尔提出的管理五大功能"计划、组织、指挥、协调、控制"至今仍被认为是管理的核心要义，沟通是实现管理职能的重要工具。

Henri Fayol's Five Main Functions of Management

(1) Planning. Planning is a decision-making process. Managers are supposed to consider the resources available in the organization and the flexibility of the personnel when they develop an outline of things to be done.

(2) Organizing. Providing capital, personnel and raw materials for the day-to-day running of the business. Organizing is to focus on how to achieve objectives.

(3) Commanding. Commanding encompasses instructing your team and making sure that the team is motivated to implement what needs to be done with rewards.

(4) Coordinating. Coordinating is all about harmonizing all activities and ensuring everything works well together.

(5) Controlling. Controlling is to confirm whether the process corresponds with plan through controlling the objectives, people and actions.

(Adapted from: Fayol, H. General and Industrial Management[M]. Dunod et E. Pinat, 1917)

Fayol's "14 Principles" was one of the earliest theories of management to be created, and remains one of the most comprehensive. He is considered to be an influential contributors to the modern concept of management.

法约尔的"14条原则"是最早系统性提出的管理理论之一，他被认为是现代管理理念的重要贡献者。

Fayol's "14 Principles"

(1) Division of Work. When employees are specialized, output can increase because they become increasingly skilled and efficient.

(2) Authority. Managers must have the authority to give orders, but they must also keep in mind that with authority comes responsibility.

(3) Discipline. Discipline must be upheld in organizations, but methods for doing so can vary.

(4) Unity of Command. Employees should have only one direct supervisor.

(5) Unity of Direction. Teams with the same objective should be working under the direction of one manager, using one plan. This will ensure that action is properly coordinated.

(6) Subordination of Individual Interests to the General Interest. The interests of one employee should not be allowed to become more important than those of the group. This includes managers.

(7) Remuneration. Employee satisfaction depends on fair remuneration for everyone. This includes financial and non-financial compensation.

(8) Centralization. This principle refers to how close employees are to the decision-making process. It is important to aim for an appropriate balance.

(9) Scalar Chain. Employees should be aware of where they stand in the organization's hierarchy, or chain of command.

(10) Order. The workplace facilities must be clean, tidy and safe for employees. Everything should have its place.

(11) Equity. Managers should be fair to staff at all times, both maintaining discipline as necessary and acting with kindness where appropriate.

(12) Stability of Tenure of Personnel. Managers should strive to minimize employee turnover. Personnel planning should be a priority.

(13) Initiative. Employees should be given the necessary level of freedom to create and carry out plans.

(14) Esprit de Corps. Organizations should strive to promote team spirit and unity.

Hierarchy presents itself in any given organization. This varies from senior management (executive board) to the lowest levels in the organization. Henri Fayol's "hierarchy" management principle states that there should be a clear line in the area of authority (from top to bottom and all managers at all levels). This can

法约尔奠基性的管理学理论——"14条原则"中，"等级链"是企业内部一条从上到下不会断裂的链条，是组织内部上下级信息传递的渠道。

be seen as a type of management structure. Each employee can contact a manager or a superior in an emergency situation without challenging the hierarchy, especially when it concerns reports about calamities to the immediate managers/superiors.

2. Elton Mayo: Human Relations Management

Elton Mayo (1880-1949) is considered the founder of the Human Relations Theory. In the year of 1924, Professor Mayo started an experiment in the Hawthorne plants, where research was conducted into changing working conditions.

Different from Scientific Management Theory, which mainly focused on productivity, efficient division of labor and workers as an extension of machinery, Human Relations Theory studied work relations in a different sight; they were now seen as thinking beings with needs, who liked to receive attention. Companies realized that attention motivated employees and even allowed them to get more out of themselves for the benefit of the organization.

In the era of the Human Relations Theory, the concept of "labor motivation" is given a new meaning compared to the Scientific Management era. Attention, respect, interest shown and social/interpersonal relationships are just as important.

3. Shannon-Weaver Model

Shannon and Weaver model is the most popular model of communication and is widely accepted all over the world. This model takes

2. 梅奥：人际关系管理

与科学管理理论关注生产力、有效分工不同，人际关系管理理论的代表人物梅奥教授提出了"社会人的假设"。

关注、尊重、兴趣和社会人际关系被看作"工作动机"的构成部分，相比科学管理时代有了新的意义。

沟通作为提高工作绩效的重要工具受到研究重视。

3. 香农-韦弗模型

借助代码传递信息的思想，香农-韦弗模型概括了人类交际的一般模式，实际上

communication as a two-way process, from the executives to the employees and also from the employees to the executives. The sender produces a message and sends it to the receiver through a technological channel and by the help of the transmitter.

Shannon and Weaver model is a transmission model consisting of five elements: an information source, which produces a message; a transmitter, which encodes the message into signals; a channel, to which signals are adapted for transmission; a receiver, which decodes (reconstructs) the message from the signal; a destination, where the message arrives. A sixth element, noise, is a dysfunctional factor: any interference with the message travelling along the channel (such as static on the telephone or radio) which may lead to the signal received being different from that sent.

是将人类复杂的交际行为简单概括为编码—传递—解码的过程。

该模型由五个要素组成：产生信息的信息源；将信息编码为信号的发送器；适合信号传输的信道；解码（重构）信息的接收器；以及信息到达的目的地。另外，噪声作为可能存在的第六个要素，是信息传输中的任何干扰因素，会导致接收到的信号与发送的信号不同。

4. Peter F. Drucker's Communication Principles

Peter F. Drucker (1909–2005), the founder of modern management, has raised the following four fundamental communication principles.

4. 彼得·德鲁克的沟通原则

四个基本原则：沟通是理解，沟通是期望，沟通创造需求，沟通与信息存在巨大差异却又相互依存。

Four Fundamental Communication Principles

(1) Communication is perception. First you should know your audience. Make sure the information is within the recipient's range, as that is the premise of a successful communication. Also, perception is not only passive reception of these signals, but also shaped by the recipient's learning, memory, expectation, and attention. Their comprehension will be influenced by the

"silent language," that is, the gestures, tones of voices, and the environment altogether because perception is more likely to be an experience.

(2) Communication is expectation. People always perceive what they expect to perceive. In fact, the recipient will ignore or block out the unexpected information unconsciously. So, in order to achieve effective communication, you should find out the recipient's expectation beforehand.

(3) Communication makes demands. It always demands the recipient become somebody, do something, or believe something. It always appeals to motivation. If, in other words, communication fits in with the aspirations, values and purposes of the recipient, it is powerful. But if it goes against his aspirations, his values and his motivations, it is likely not to be received at all or, at best, to be resisted.

(4) Communication and information are different and indeed largely opposite — yet interdependent. As we have learned in the models of communication, information is always encoded. To be received — let alone to be used, the code must be known and understood by the recipient. The validity of information depends on the pre-establishment of communication.

5. The Theory of Kenneth Burke

The "Pentad" of Kenneth Burke (1897-1993) contains five elements: agent, act, scene, agency, purpose. Communication is defined as "an agent acts in a particular scene through specific agencies to achieve a particular goal".

Agent (Our Source): An agent is usually a person or a group or any entity to choose whether or not to perform certain acts. Focusing on agent is particularly appropriate when addressing issues like staffing, motivation, working relationships, training programs, and personnel development. A clear explanation from an agent-centered

5. 伯克的沟通"五因素"理论

行动者在特殊场景下借助特定的媒介实现某项具体的目标。

行动者（信息源）是能够选择是否实施某种行为的个体或群体。基于行动者视角，受众最关注的问题"我是如何受到影响的？"将会得到解答。

perspective can answer your audience's crucial question: How does this affect me?

Act (Strategy and Tactics): Act can include anything you do to achieve a goal and it always involves designing and deliver specific communications. Focusing on act needs to consider the important details of implementation: who should do what, in what way, in what order, at what time. This is the language of instruction kits, operating manuals, and implementation sections of an action plan. When used well, an act-centered approach can provide a road map for reaching the goal.

行动（策略和手段）是包括"谁该以什么方式、什么顺序、什么时间、做什么事"等具体的行动计划。

Scene (Context): Scene refers to the setting for agents, acts and other variables in a decision. It includes governmental regulations, media attention, social issues, and political developments in the global marketplace.

场景指的是一项决策中行动者、行动和其他变量发生作用的背景和环境。

Goal: Focusing on communication goal helps a communicator to explain how individuals and groups will benefit from achieving the goal. It is a persuasive way to emphasize the goal if you want to ask someone to take an act.

关注目标将会帮助行动者更好地说服受众采取行动。

Agency (Mostly Messages): It means the tools to accomplish your act. It includes materials, processes, skills, human resources and ways of motivating people to do things. Choosing the right message to send and the right medium to send it, becomes crucial to achieving your goal. An appropriate agency-centered approach can ensure that the systems are in place to achieve the desired result. Otherwise it can over-emphasize technical, mechanical, or procedural matters.

媒介指完成行动的一切手段和资源。不仅包括资料、流程、技能、人力资源，也包括激励人们做事的方法。选择合适的媒介发布信息对于实现目标具有重要影响。

1.3 Elements of Communication

When we are the source, we are the people who send messages to our audience in a specific context through the chosen media so as to achieve some objectives and to provoke a response. The above process includes seven elements for a complete communication, which help us better understand the tangibles and intangibles behind the art of communication (See Figure 1.1).

三、沟通要素

沟通七要素——沟通者、目标、听众、情境、信息、媒介、反馈。

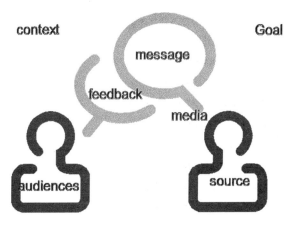

Figure 1.1　Elements of Communication
图 1.1　七大沟通要素

Source: The source is the person who attempts to share information. As a qualified sender, you should always ask yourself, "Why should he or she trust me?" And try to be credible, effective, and persuadable.

Goal: The goals of communication often vary a lot. What do you intend to achieve after you finish the conversation? How to make it clear

沟通者是信息的发布源，要做到可信、有效、有说服力。

目标是指需要实现的特定结果。

enough to carry out? And how you access or evaluate success? Some goals may seem obvious at first, but when you weight them against the costs, especially after reality check, you might find that the goals need to be redefined.

Audience: Get to know your audience before the communication starts. What do they already know? Have your any shared value or common ground? Is their attitude positive, neutral or negative? Also, pay attention to the secondary audiences and hidden audiences. As the founder of modern management science, Peter Drucker once said, "To improve communication, work not on the utterer, but the recipient."

听众是你的沟通对象。在沟通前需要对你的听众做深入细致的了解和分析。

Context: Communication are better understood in a specific context. And the environment can be divided into two categories: internal and external environment. If you take the change of the environment for granted, you will be influenced and constrained by it. The main context of communication includes social background, psychological background, physical background, and culture background.

沟通是在特定情境中发生的，包括社会环境、心理情境、物理情境和文化背景等。

Message: To achieve your goals with different types of audience, it's of vital importance to make your message accessible and persuasive. Successful message design depends on content (what you have to say) and argument (how you build your persuasive case).

信息是沟通最为核心的部分，包括信息的内容和信息的论证方式。

Feedback: Feedback is a response from the receiver that informs the sender how the communication is being received in general. It is inevitably essential in case of two-way

沟通是一个双向互动的过程，沟通者通过反馈可以了解沟通的效果，并采取进一步策略。

communication that enables you to know the reaction of audience as well as make the audience feel more involved in the process.

Media: We use many ways and channels of communication in order to convey the message effectively to our audience. In fact, the information technology practically eliminated the physical costs of communications. Besides the traditional media, such as face-to-face communication, phone calls, letters, files, conferences, newspapers and magazines, new media, such as emails, microblog, WeChat, is widely used in modern communication.

媒介是信息的传递渠道，随着科技进步越来越多的传播媒介被创造出来。

Exercise:
Suppose you are a project manager who wants to persuade your superior to invest more in your project. Consider what are the seven elements in communication analysis.

小练习：
假设你是公司的一位项目经理，想说服你的上级追加项目投资。思考一下沟通的七个基本要素包括什么？

1.4 Why Management Communication Is Important

四、管理沟通的重要性

Managers spend more time on communication than on anything else. The companies that have problems in communication, will inevitably result in weak performance of human resources and other problems. Communication problems have become so diverse and prominent that in modern companies, they are considered as the top

管理沟通在现代管理中至关重要，沟通存在问题的企业将在人力资源管理、领导力等方面遇到困难。

priorities.

From the perspective of management objects, the essence of management is the integration of various resources. Therefore, it is necessary for managers to establish an effective and strong link amongst them. This requires a bridge of connections, and communication is the bridge that enables the effective connections between information.

管理是将各种资源进行整合。因此，管理者需要在各要素间架起沟通的桥梁。

Communication is also critical to managers in terms of managerial functions. Managers are the people that organize, command, lead, coordinate and control other people to make sure they complete their work correctly and achieve their goals. All the functions can't work without communication.

从管理职能的角度，管理者需要通过沟通来组织、命令、领导、协调、控制其他人完成相应的工作，从而达成目标。

This book provides business students with rationale of management communication. To help them better understand and apply the knowledge they have learned, there are also some cases in real business situations in each chapter to guide your analysis. While trenchant analysis provides the crucial underpinnings for a successful communication process, only practice can ensure that effective communication becomes second nature to you as a manager.

本书将为学生提供管理沟通的有效工具方法，掌握管理沟通的理论知识和实践技能。

◇【Conclusion】本章小结

In this chapter, we reviewed research developments on management communication, from scientific management, human relations management to modern management theories. We discussed the basic elements of communication, including source, goal, context, audience, message, media and feedback.

【Study Questions】课后问题

1. Why is communication of great importance in many management situations?
2. What are the research developments in each stage from scientific management theory to modern management?
3. What are the seven elements of communication?

Chapter 2   Source: How to be a Successful Communicator

第 2 章   如何做一个成功的沟通者

As a communicator, you are the person who intends to convey the message to your audiences. You should consider why you are the most appropriate person to make the communication? Why should you be trusted? How to increase your credibility?

In this chapter, you will:
- learn the qualities you should have as a communicator;
- use the knowledge you have learned to be more credible when communicating.

沟通者需要向听众传递信息，你需要考虑为何你是进行沟通最合适的人？你为什么值得信任？如何增强可信度？

学习本章，你将会了解作为沟通者应该具备的品质；利用所学的技能增加沟通的可信度。

2.1   Goodwill

一、良好意愿

"Of the modes of persuasion furnished by the spoken word there are three kinds. The first kind depends on the personal character of the speaker [ethos]; the second on putting the audience into a certain frame of mind [pathos]; the third on the proof, or apparent proof, provided by the words of the speech itself [logos]. Persuasion is achieved by the speaker's personal character when the speech is so spoken as to make us think him credible." In the book *Rhetoric*, Aristotle defined three essential qualities of successful communication: logos,

亚里士多德就认识到情感对于沟通效果的重要作用，在其巨作《修辞学》中提出了属于技术范围的三种基本说服方式：人品诉求（ethos）、情感诉求（pathos）和理性诉求（logos）。他指出，沟通者需要提高自己的可信度，以提升个人魅力。

pathos, and ethos. He further defined emotion as states of mind involving pleasure and pain, which in return influence our perceptions.

These perceptions bring up an important concept: goodwill is beneficial to successful communication. Goodwill means showing your attention and respects to others. It has been widely validated by current experience that goodwill plays a critical role in management communication.

"良好意愿"是指对沟通对象抱有的善意和敬意，对提高沟通效果具有重要影响。

2.2 You-Attitude

1. Three Conceived Positions in Communication

二、换位思考

1. 沟通中的三个感知位置

Different men usually see the same subject in different lights. Also, in each communication situation, there are three conceived positions to the communicator: oneself, counterpart and third parties (See Figure 2.1):

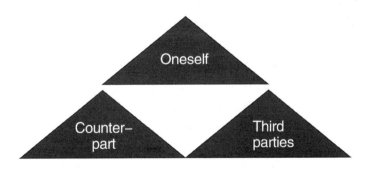

Figure 2.1　The Three Conceived Positions in Communication
图2.1　沟通中的三个感知位置

These three conceived positions provide us with the perspectives of thinking when

换位思考是指沟通者善于在自己、沟通对象、其他

communicating with others. Some people can only see or understand things from one perspective — the "oneself" perspective, while some people can position himself or herself in other positions such as his or her counterpart and third parties. We also need to emphasize that no single point of view is the "completely correct" view. In fact, all opinions, even if they are correct, cannot be complete. Therefore, only by observing from all viewpoints can we get a better understanding. The ability to switch thinking positions in communication is a crucial advantage for a successful communicator.

(1) First position: oneself.

From the "oneself" point of view, the person is self-centered and possessed with personal thoughts and needs. This perspective can be used for self-awareness, self-reflection and self-exploration, so that you can understand yourself and deliver your thoughts better. However, we human beings are initiated with self-centered behavior, we tend to see things from our own points of view. If a person only takes this position in communication, it will make others think he/she is somehow selfish, ignorant of the situation and other people's feelings, which may cause conflictions in communication.

(2) Second position: counterpart.

Empathy is a way of thinking about what other people think, understanding each other, trusting, and learning to empathize. For a manager, the ability to empathize is an important

人这三个感知位置之间不断切换，通过把自己想象成不同角色，增进对事物的理解和感知，从而从不同的维度思考要弄清的问题，提高沟通效果。

（1）第一个感知位置是"自我"位置。

从自我角度出发看待事物可以增强自我意识、自我反馈和自我发现，但是如果在沟通中一直站在这个立场，会让对方产生自我中心感过强的不愉悦感觉，进而导致沟通失败。

（2）第二个感知位置是"沟通对象"位置。

优秀的管理者善于通过"移情"增进管理沟通效果。当然，过度行为也容易导致

factor in the success of management. But if stocked in this position, a person will think too much before making decisions thus may cause delay of action.

(3) Third position: third parties.

The third parties' perspective demands objectivity, neutrality, remaining observers or outsiders. We use it as a rational objective analysis to obtain objective conclusions. This position will allow the communicator to keep a rational, indifferent, and impersonal attitude in communication.

2. You-Attitude

"You-attitude" refers to a style of writing that puts readers' needs first, stated by Kitty O. Locker in *Business and Administrative Communication*, and it also can be applied in daily communication. Communication styles could be dramatically different between with you-attitude and without you-attitude.

瞻前顾后、决策迟缓。

（3）第三个感知位置是"他人"位置。

通过置于第三方的感知位置，沟通者可以客观、置身事外地对沟通内容进行理解和感知。

2. 换位思考

换位思考可以增进沟通效果。通过对比以下示例中是否使用换位思考的不同效果，可以增强对"换位思考"原则的理解。

---

(1) Talk about your audience, not about yourself.
强调听众利益，而非自己的利益。
Without you-attitude: I will greatly benefit from your task.
You-attitude: All of our team members will benefit from you doing this task.

(2) Refer to your audience's request or order specifically.
将听众的要求具体化表达。
Without you-attitude: According to your request, we have already revised the draft design.
You-attitude: We have already changed the color from brown to blue as you requested.

(3) Use *you* more often than *I* in positive situations.

在积极的事物方面强调"你"（听众）。

Without you-attitude: I'll walk you through a guidebook that will show you how to write your own proposal.

You-attitude: You will learn the skills on how to write a proposal after I walk you through the guidebook.

(4) **Avoid the word *you* in delivering bad news, as it can be interpreted as accusatory and over-accentuate the negative.**

在消极情境或传达负面消息时，尽量避免使用"你"以减弱负面对立效果。

Without you-attitude: You failed in hitting the target this quarter.

You-attitude: Unfortunately, the target of this quarter is not achieved.

2.3 Credibility

1. Communicator's Credibility: the Process of Trust Building

Credibility is defined as believability, trustworthiness, dependability, and one's integrity. Some even consider it as the power to inspire others to act, to do, to behave and to respond in certain ways. In business communication, it is essential that the communicator is regarded as credible and trustworthy. The audiences evaluate your credibility by what you say, how you say it, what they see you doing and what they think your intention is. However, with the increasingly rapid economic globalization, enormous changes within organizations as well as in external environment promote uncertainty among employees. When communicating in business, the credibility

三、增加可信度

1. 沟通者可信度：建立信任的过程

可信度是影响沟通效果的重要因素，特别是在当今复杂的商业环境下，随着不确定性的增强，沟通者的可信度对于有效沟通尤为重要。

of communicators influences the attitudes of audience towards you and your idea.

In Reasons for trust, Zerfass[1] proposed the features of high trust value, and gave the principles of building credits in communication.

(1) Adequacy of communication.

It is necessary for managers to communicate with employees at regular intervals, which not only helps them keep consistency of ideas but also reach a consensus on one aspect. However, the frequency of communication should be moderate. Over-communication is a waste of resource, which will despite all your efforts and bore your audiences.

(2) Consistency of communication.

Pay attention to the consistency of the content and methods when communicating. In order to achieve effective communication, communicators must consider the historical situation, because people respond to various situations based on their own experiences, emotions and expectations. Maintaining a certain continuity will help your audiences to accurately understand the connotation of communication.

(3) Openness of communication.

Be frank to your audiences. The model of Johari Window in the attachment further explained the importance of being openness to your audiences.

构建沟通者可信度的原则包括沟通的充分性、一致性、公开性，以及符合社会道德准则。

（1）沟通的充分性。

管理者与员工应有规律地进行沟通，既保证一定的频率能够把事情交流清楚，又不过度。

（2）沟通的一致性。

沟通应考虑过去已有的沟通内容，以及与其他不同听众的沟通内容的一致性。

（3）沟通的公开性。

对听众坦诚、公开（见本章附录"约哈里窗户"）。

---

1 Zerfass, A. Corporate Communication Revisited: Integrating Business Strategy and Strategic Communication[J]. Public Relations Research, 2008.

(4) Social responsibility and ethic of responsibility.

It often reflects in the concept of your communication. A concept runs from beginning to end in a communication and governs all the constituent parts. If the concept of the communication supports social and ethic responsibility, your audiences are more inclined to believe you.

2. Types of Credibility

The concept of credibility could be categorized into three groups: initial credibility, derived credibility and terminal credibility. In the process of credibility building, we need to pay attention to the features of each group. The more credibility we build, the more effectiveness we may gain in communication.

Initial credibility — the credibility an individual has before he or she begins to speak — this type of credibility may be the result of the speaker's position, expertise, or simply the fact that he/she was asked to speak.

Derived credibility — the credibility an individual creates through what he/she has to say — this type of credibility may stem from the speaker's ability to communicate, the speaker's ideas, or the information he/she uses to support his or her position.

Terminal credibility — the credibility an individual has when he/she finishes speaking — this type of credibility is often a result of the other two types and influences the impact of the

（4）沟通的社会责任和道德责任。

沟通应建立在尊重社会道德责任的基础上，以获得听众的认同。

2. 可信度的类型

可信度可以分为三种基本类型：初始可信度、派生可信度、最终可信度。

初始可信度是指沟通者与生俱来或已经具有的特质，如职位地位、专业等级、外表形象等。

派生可信度是指沟通者在沟通期间所说和所做的一切产生的可信度，其受到沟通质量和沟通者专业性的影响。

最终可信度是指沟通者在与听众沟通后，沟通者获得的印象。最终可信度比派生可信度更加持久。

message (i.e., will the listeners adopt a long-term change).

3. How to Increase Credibility in Communication

Factors such as rank, goodwill, expertise, image and common ground will influence credibility building. Some people possess favorable initial credibility, while others need to strengthen afterwards. You can stress your initial credibility by emphasizing your title, rank, position, expertise, etc. and increase acquired credibility by creating a connection between you and people with higher credibility.

3. 如何增加沟通的可信度

在身份地位、专业程度、形象、共同价值观等影响可信度的诸多要素中，某些人先天具备初始可信度，而其他人则需要通过强调职务、头衔、职位、专业等增加后天可信度。

Example:
When you apply for future study in a university, in addition to your CV or resume, you probably need to provide some recommendations. A referee with higher status, expertise or knowledge is more favorable to the candidate. The recommendation is a connection which helps to increase acquired credibility.

Credibility is affected by the interaction of both sides. Involve your audience when you are speaking, share them with the interests, visions, and to make them feel co-oriented to "common grounds".

In the book of *Guide to Managerial Communication*, Mary Munter explained the techniques for credibility building (See Table 2.1).

增进彼此互动也可以增进可信度，与听众分享你的兴趣、目标等有助于建立共同的价值观。

Table 2.1 Factors and Techniques for Credibility
表2.1 可信度的影响因素与方法

Factor	Based on ...	Stress initial credibility by ...	Increase acquired credibility by ...
Rank	Hierarchical power	Emphasizing your title or rank	Associating yourself with or citing a high-ranking person (e.g., by his or her cover letter or introduction)
Goodwill	Personal relationship or "track record"	Referring to relationship or "track record"	Building your goodwill by emphasizing audience benefits, "what's in it for them"
Goodwill	Trustworthiness	Offering balanced evaluation; acknowledging any conflict of interest	
Expertise	Knowledge, competence	Sharing your expert understanding Explaining how you gained your expertise	Associating yourself with or citing authoritative sources
Image	Attractiveness, audience's desire to be like you	Emphasizing attributes audience finds attractive	Associating yourself with high-image people
Image	Authenticity, sincerity	Communicating openly, sincerely connecting with audience, showing appropriate emotion	
Common ground	Common values, ideas, problems, or needs	Establishing your shared values or ideas Acknowledging similarities with audience Tying the message to your common ground	

【Conclusion】本章小结

Goodwill is beneficial to successful communication. Goodwill means to show your attention and respects to others. There are three conceived positions to the communicator: oneself, the counter-part and third parties. Credibility is the quality of being believed or trusted, which is crucial for communication management.

Adequacy, consistency, transparency, openness, social responsibility and ethic of responsibility are basic features in building communication credits.

Credibility could be categorized into three groups: initial credibility, derived credibility and terminal credibility. Initial credibility is built on rank, goodwill, expertise, image and common ground. The communicator needs to increase credibility in communicating.

【Reading Material】Johari Window 约哈里窗户

Possessing reliable initial credibility is lucky. However, if a communicator has limited experience or is too young to be trusted in the first place, how to gain credibility to make a successful communication?

The theory of Johari Window may shed some light.

The theory of Johari Window is a technique invented by psychologists Joseph Luft and Harrington Ingham, which helps people better understand their relationship with themselves and others. And there are four quadrants: Open area, blind area, hidden area and unknown area (See Figure 2.2).

Open area：The area is known by the person about himself and is also known by others. The reason why you can't get trust quickly from your audiences is because the open area is too small to be understood by others. Therefore, in order to gain trust, expand the open area first and let your audience get to know you as soon as possible.

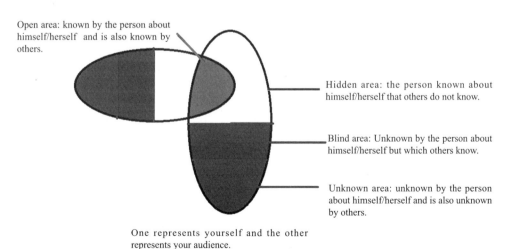

Figure 2.2　Johari Window
图 2.2　约哈里窗户

These include your own strengths and small flaws.

Blind area: It is unknown by the person about him/herself but which others know. Get feedback and seek advice from your audience. Finding your own shortcomings is a quick way to improve yourselves and make the next communication better.

Hidden area: The area is what the person knows about himself/herself that others do not know. Minimize this area as much as possible. The communicator who is too mysterious can't get trust from others especially when you are a new person here.

Unknown area: It is unknown by the person about himself/herself and is also unknown by others. To get recognition from others, you must find your core strengths, and constantly develop your potential.

Johari Window is not static but dynamic, and we can change the distribution of the four color chips of the window by our efforts. So how can we cooperate and communicate more effectively with people in the business? The answer is to reduce the blind area and hidden area, striving to expand the open area and trying to explore the unknown area.

In most cases, people are used to showing their strengths and concealing their own disadvantages and deficiencies. Sometimes, if you get that turned around, and properly expose your weaknesses to others, you can win the trust and respect of them.

The psychologist Arthur Aron thinks, "One key pattern associated with the development of a close relationship among peers is sustained, escalating, reciprocal, personal self-disclosure." He did a study that explores whether intimacy between two strangers can be accelerated by having them ask each other a specific series of personal questions. According to his theory, there are four levels of self-exposure. The first level is your interests, such as hobbies, lifestyles, and so on. The second level is about your attitudes, such as your attitudes or opinions on the government or a specific thing. The third level is about self-awareness and interpersonal relationships, such as your own emotions, relationships with family, friends, and so on. The fourth level is about privacy, such as your own secrets, attitudes, ideas and behaviors that are not accepted by society.

【Case Study】案例讨论

The Future of an Excellent Staff

Alfred P. Sloan Jr. (1875–1966) was an innovative leader of General Motors during the early twentieth. He served as the company's CEO and president. In his book, *My Years with General Motors*, he mentioned a moment of communication:

"During the years, the production line of Cadillac was in trouble. The brand didn't make profit as expected and became a big burden of GM group. When the board of directors was having a meeting to vote the future of Cadillac, i.e. to keep it or to cut it, an engineer from Cadillac entered the meeting room without invitation. He delivered an inspiring speech on the optimistic prospects of Cadillac in the hope that the company would keep the production line. Following the impassioned speech was a long silence. Board members didn't know what to say to the loyal engineer. Then, slowly, Sloan said, we understand your feelings and your loyalty to this brand. Even if Cadillac fails, I will find you another position in GM group, because your consideration is with the future of Cadillac, while my consideration is with the..."

Questions:

1. What would Mr. Sloan say? What intention did he want to convey to the engineer?
2. After listening to Sloan, how would the engineer feel and act?

【Study Questions】课后问题

1. Discuss the advantages and disadvantages of three conceived positions when communicating.
2. How to improve credibility as a communicator?

Chapter 3　Setting Goals
第3章　设定沟通目标

Differing from lunching or socializing with friends in daily life, managerial communication is targeted on achieving specific results. This chapter focuses on establishing achievable goals within a particular context. In business, the managers often need to deal with many communication decisions simultaneously. The right decision on one task often involves the wrong decision on another. Before communication happens, the manager must define priorities. For each communication case, the managers are expected to make an appropriate strategy, set clear goals, assess the context, design a course of action to ensure that the communication is fruitful.

In this chapter, you will:
- understand the SMART principle in setting goals;
- learn to categorize goals into strategic goals, tactic goals and task goals;
- learn to test context according to urgency and importance.

3.1　Setting SMART Goals

You have a much greater chance of accomplishing a specific goal than a general goal.

与生活中日常沟通不同，管理沟通的目的是要实现特定的结果。管理者常常同时面对诸多沟通问题，需要合理确定优先级，制定沟通计划与目标，评估情境，作出行动计划，以期沟通目标能够顺利达成。

学习本章，你将会了解设定目标的SMART原则；学会将目标分为策略目标、战术目标、任务目标；根据紧迫性与重要性进行情境分析。

一、设定目标

SMART目标设定原则对于有效沟通至关重要，指目

In managerial situations, such as fixing a problem; get your proposal adopted; have a meeting with your sales team, using SMART principle to set goals is of great importance to effective communication. SMART refers to Specific, Measurable, Attainable, Relevant and Time-based in developing goals.

1. Setting Your Goal Specific

Someone would say, "I hope to become a successful manager in the future." It could be regarded as a goal in career development, but it's too vague to be carried out. If it is optimized as "I hope to get the marketing manager position within 5 years through increasing my sales performance skills of management communication", then it's time to analyze the context in which you are trying to achieve and use process approach (which will be mentioned below) to define and accomplish the subsidiary goals.

标的具体性（S）、可测量性（M）、可实现性（A）、相关性（R）和时间性（T）。

1. 目标的"具体性"

SMART原则的第一个要求是"具体"。通过7个W层层发问，可以帮助你认清你的目标是模糊还是具体。

Seven Ws to Make a Specific Goal

What? Ask what specifically you want to accomplish. This is the basic question of what goal you hope to achieve. It needs to be a concrete, specific goal that can be measured.

Where? Determine where this will happen. Identify a location in which you will do the work of striving for your goal.

How? Determine how to reach your goal. Evaluate and choose between different methods to achieve your goal.

When? Think about when this will happen. Establish a realistic time frame or deadline for achieving your goal.

> Who? Determine who is involved. Not only the ones taking actions, but also the ones who will be affected.
>
> What are the conditions and limitations? Identify which requirements and restraints as well as obstacles will be part of the process, such as, what will you need to do to achieve your goal? What obstacles will you face?
>
> Why? Why this way? Why should I be the communicator? Are there any other possible ways or persons to do the task?

2. Making Your Goal Measurable

To evaluate the achievements, managers should make their goals measurable. Develop criteria on measuring outcomes, from both quantitative (numbers based) and descriptive (based on describing a certain outcome) perspectives. Ask yourself questions to clarify, until the goal is as measurable as possible.

In most cases, concrete numbers are helpful in measuring your goals, since you'll know without question if you're falling behind or if you're on track. Then, you need to track and measure your progress. Keep a journal can help you keep things in perspective and can also release stress you might be feeling about your efforts.

3. Making Sure the Goal Is Attainable

You want to make sure that the goal you have set can be achieved. Otherwise, you may become discouraged. A goal that can never be achieved is meaningless. Acknowledge your limitations honestly. Identify the restraints and obstacles you might have run across and how you'll deal with

2. 目标的"可测量性"

目标的"可测量性"要求管理者制定明确的"标准"以检验目标达成与否。通过提问来帮助你找到尽可能能实现的目标，可以是定量的，也可以是定性的。

具体的数字有助于衡量你的目标，并通过跟踪和测量进度以确保目标达成。

3. 目标的"可实现性"

目标应该具有可实现性，否则将失去制定目标的意义。应该坦诚地面对自己在能力、知识、时间等方面的局限性，并可以记录下来以便更清楚地面对。

them is crucial to achieving your goals.

Assess your level of commitment. Your goal and your commitment level should match up. Even if a goal is theoretically achievable, you must be committed to making the efforts necessary to reach it. Be honest with yourself about the changes you are willing to make.

如实评估对目标的投入程度，目标设定应该与投入程度相匹配。

Are you prepared to make the commitment to reach your target? Are you willing to dramatically alter or at least adjust aspects of your life? If not, is there a more achievable target you are willing to work for? Once you've considered the challenges you face and your level of commitment, adjust your goal as necessary. This doesn't mean you have to give up altogether. It just means adjusting your goal to fit your reality.

全面衡量挑战，合理调整设定的目标。

Tips and Advices

Evaluate challenges you might face, and identify actions you can take to overcome these potential obstacles. The question to consider here is whether it's reasonable to think you'll be able to accomplish the goal in the face of these challenges.

Be realistic about the amount of time available to devote to your goals with your personal background, knowledge, and any physical limitations.

Write down all the foreseeable constraints you face as you make this assessment. This will help you develop complete picture of the task you face.

4. Making Your Goal Relevant

Closely related to a goal's attainability is its relevance. Managers face many communication

4. 目标的"相关性"

与目标的可实现性密切相关的是它的相关性。管理

decisions simultaneously, and sometimes there are apparent contradictions between different decisions. Does this goal seem worthwhile? Does this match other efforts in the team? Make connection between different goals and the main goal.

Reflect on your desires. It is time to revisit the "why" question at this step. Ask yourself whether this goal will truly fulfill your desires or if there's a different goal that's more important to you.

Consider your other goals and circumstances. It's also important to consider how your goal fits with other plans in the picture of a whole business. Conflicting plans can create problems. Adjust your goal for relevance.

5. Making the Goal Time-Based

Goals must have a clear deadline to work toward, which benefits avoiding procrastination. Having intermediate goals can be set at weekly or monthly intervals, depending on the time frame for the main goal.

Choose a time frame. Setting a timeline for your goal helps you identify and stick to the specific actions that you need to take to work towards that goal.

Set benchmarks. It can be useful to break your goal up into smaller ones, especially if your goal is a very long-term one. This can help you measure your progress and make it manageable.

Focus on the long term and the short term. Often, focusing on specific short-term goals can blind you to the bigger picture. Consistent

者同时面临许多沟通决策，有时不同决策之间存在明显的矛盾。这个目标是否值得？这是否与团队中的其他工作相匹配？需要把不同的目标和主要目标联系起来。

设定的目标是否与终极目标及现有的其他目标相冲突？考虑目标如何与其他计划相适应也是很重要的。

在对环境准确评估的基础上再一次调整设定的目标。

5. 目标的"时间性"

目标必须有明确的工作期限，这有助于避免拖延。根据主要目标的时间框架，可以每周或每月设置中间目标。

设定合理的时间表和目标进度要求，以便在工作中推进执行。尤其需要将长期目标分解成更小的分阶段目标，以便衡量进度并使其易于管理。

同时，应注意平衡短期目标和长期目标的关系。

progress toward your goals means keeping one eye on today and the other eye on the future. You may need to ask yourself: What can I do today to reach my goal? And the next 3 weeks? And over the long run? The good manager knows how to hold a principled vision while making informed choices among a number of specific options.

3.2 Sorting Goals

You're more likely to achieve goals that are SMART. In business context, managers can best sort the goals according to whether they are strategies, tactics, or tasks.

The goal of strategy represents the real business goal. It is helpful to write down your primary business goal and always keep in mind during your planning.

二、目标的分类

按照策略、方案、任务将目标进行分类。

策略性目标指真正的商业目标。在策略性目标之下,管理者可以制定战术目标和任务目标。

Example:

In order to increase market share, the new product needs to attain higher availability and visibility.

Under the guidance of strategy goal, managers can break down the primary goals into tactics and tasks. When you set goals, communicate them clearly to your staffs, and identify specific ways that your team can achieve your desired outcomes. Your employees need to be up to date about your business goals in order to achieve them.

当设定目标时,需要与下属进行具体的沟通。

Secondarily, the manager needs to determine goals of tactics, which means that after setting a clear business goal, he or she should identify the specific

将最终的商业目标分解成一系列子目标,即具体的战术方案,这是实现目标的

actions needed to achieve your desired outcome. For example, in order to attain higher availability and visibility, the company needs to acquire new outlets and increase advertising budget.

These actions are necessary to achieve your business goal. What do you expect your staffs to do? Clear tactic plan will keep your staffs' awareness.

Next, managers need to plan step-by-step tasks that most likely to achieve your secondary goals. These are tertiary or communication goals, which may involve managerial activities like persuading an individual, holding a meeting, writing a proposal, etc. For example, in order to acquire new outlets and increase advertising budget, the company needs to develop budget proposal and location research for starting new outlets; develop advertising and public relations proposals for launching new products.

Sorting goals is a bunch of processes including setting real business goal (strategy), and then breaking it down into specific subsidiary goals (tactics), followed by a set of communication goals (tasks), such as writing up proposals, conducting interviews, calling staff meetings to increase awareness and allocate works. Clearly sorting the goals will help managers to balance the long-run and the short-run in business, without letting the means become the ends.

行动路线。

明确一系列具体的行动任务，也可以看作沟通任务。通过沟通实现团队协作，以实现最终商业目标的达成。

在整个计划过程中，管理者应始终牢记商务（战略）目标、方案（战术）目标和任务（沟通/行动）目标之间的区分。

3.3 Context Testing by Defining Urgency and Importance

三、基于紧迫性和重要性进行情境分析

It is not only necessary but also of great

情境分析对于设定目标

importance to test your goals against the context in which you're trying to achieve them. Context testing not only includes your personal position, such as knowledge, interests, title, time limitation, and quality of relationship within organizations, but also includes reasonable defining of urgency and importance upon the simultaneously aroused tasks.

In order to get the priority right of our tasks, and select those important things from trivial matters, managers are ought to master the skill of time management. An Urgent Important Matrix is a simple but effective tool for prioritizing the to-do list based on the level of urgency and importance of each task. This method also works in goals setting (See Figure 3.1).

非常重要。情境分析不仅包括组织中个人的地位、知识、兴趣等，也包括对事务重要性和紧迫性的判断。

重要程度—紧迫程度矩阵可以帮助我们更好地给目标分类排序。

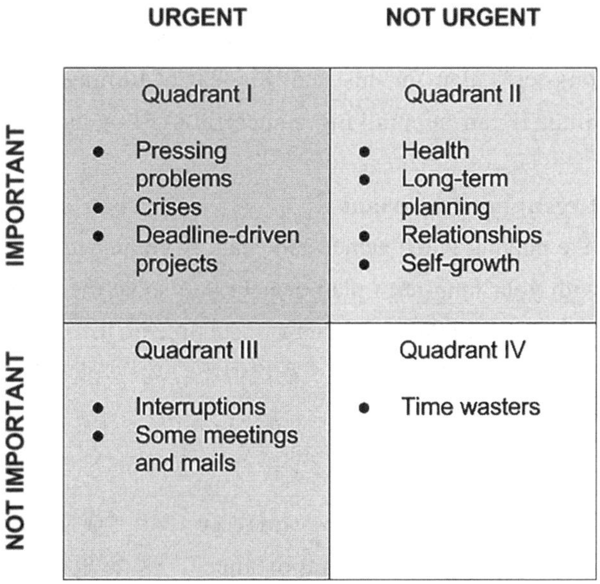

	URGENT	NOT URGENT
IMPORTANT	Quadrant I • Pressing problems • Crises • Deadline-driven projects	Quadrant II • Health • Long-term planning • Relationships • Self-growth
NOT IMPORTANT	Quadrant III • Interruptions • Some meetings and mails	Quadrant IV • Time wasters

Figure 3.1　Urgency-Importance Matrix
图 3.1　紧迫性—重要性矩阵

Urgency means the decision needs to be made immediately or the problem needs to be solved right away in case it turns to a bigger one.

紧迫性指处理该项事务的紧急程度。

The goals which benefit the achievement of real business goals are called importance. And the more beneficial to achieve business goals, the more important they are.

重要性指对实现最终商务目标的重要程度。

1. **Both Urgent and Important**

   This kind of item should be done at first and do this task will also fulfill the long-term goals of a company. It can be a crisis or a deadline to hand out a proposal.

2. **Urgent but Not Important**

   Set a time limit to finish this item to avoid it occupying too much time. It can be some unimportant phone calls or your colleagues who are seeking for help immediately.

3. **Important but Not Urgent**

   According to Covey, we should seek to spend most of our time in this part. Do a long-term plan for this item for fear of turning into the urgent and important thing. It can be studying a specific skill or making your monthly plan.

4. **Neither Urgent nor Important**

   Things like playing video games and chatting are unnecessary actions which do nothing with your long-term plan or help you solve the immediate problem. Control yourself to avoid them and don't waste time on it.

   矩阵中划分了"重要且紧迫""紧迫但不重要""重要但不紧迫",以及"不重要也不紧迫"四种情况。

Managers need to develop context analysis by defining urgency and importance when setting goals and implementing flexible work arrangements. Time constraints require

成功的管理者善于利用这个矩阵作出明智的决策。其他一些人会将很多时间投入紧迫但是不重要的事务中,

that managers do some tasks immediately while postpone others. Before communication happens, define priority according to Urgency-Importance Matrix will help managers to make accurate decisions. And in most cases, people think urgency trumps importance. Consequently, they spend too much time dealing with those urgency but unimportant things. As a manager, you should learn to empower your subordinates to manage those affairs and concentrate on the important and urgent tasks as well as invest in the important but not urgent things to prevent them becoming urgent.

从而导致疲于应付，错过最终目标。

【Conclusion】本章小结

Management communication is designed to get a specific result. In this chapter, we discussed setting SMART goals within a particular context. The goals can be categorized into strategic goal, tactic goal, or task goal.

In bushiness context, the managers must define priorities according to urgency and importance.

【Case Study】案例讨论

SMART Principle in Huawei

As one of the world-famous Chinese enterprises, Huawei has a lot of practices in following SMART principle when setting the goals.

1. Specific

Employees in Huawei work very hard and often work overtime. How to increase efficiency? Zhengfei Ren, Board Chairman of Huawei proposed "aiming before shooting", which means employees should start to work after setting goals. The individual goal should be consistent with the corporate goal, which will let employees understand what they can do to satisfy the development needs of the company. When

Huawei trains its employees, every employee must figure out the following five things before they start working: What to do? How to do it? How much? Where to do? Why? Understanding these five points helps to guide employees to do their jobs correctly.

2. Measurable

The work objectives must be clear and quantified. When performing the jobs, the employees in Huawei often follow a specific work process. There are three quantification indexes: time, quantity, quality. For example, the directly quantifiable targets such as the number of products and the number of inspections can be measured quantitatively. The indicators that cannot be directly quantified are then measured from the perspective of time and quality. For instance, the complaint rate can reflect the employees' performances; the pass rate of a document can reflect the quality of the document drafting.

The above three quantitative indexes run through the whole process of the work. With these three indexes, the employees can ensure that the work is in place. For example, when the company is conducting attendance statistics, the requirement is "Complete 15,000 attendance statistics within 3 hours, form a time sheet, and report to the executive timely." The unfinished or lack of any indexes will affect the achievement of the target. This method of work effectively ensures that the employee's work goals will not deviate too much from reality and will not be out of reach.

3. Attainable

KPI (key performance indicator) is widely used in performance management. In order to set achievable goals, Huawei always does a series of investigation, feasibility study, discuss the difficulty of the goal and evaluate whether the goal can be achieved. Zhengfei Ren holds the idea that any goal must be executable, and any lack of execution or unattainable goal is useless. Proposing unrealistic plans is not welcomed in Huawei. In their view, once the goal is out of reach, it will become a burden.

4. Time-Based

Rome was not built in a day. The development of Huawei is step by step and it's the same as the achievement of any goal, which is also reflected in the daily work. In fact, the employees in Huawei always work in strict accordance with the principle of "setting-implementing-accomplishing-setting." Taking the marketing department as an example, the salesmen usually receive tasks divided by years. How much sales volume to complete in the first year, how much to increase in the second year and the third year. Until the fifth year, what is the market share of target customer? And what is the expected market share in next decade? These will be included in the core of the work. In addition, both managers and employees will propose a short-term plan and a medium-term plan of themselves, which are usually relatively stable. Then everyone knows what they should do in the short term and long term.

Huawei has a five-year goal and a ten-year blueprint for the company. For the company departments and teams, the goals are controlled within two or three years for the short-term goals can effectively ensure the employees will not take a big leap forward.

In fact, Huaweiers often compare the development of company to a marathon. Without the clear goal and time limit, the runners can easily give up. If the runners can divide the destination with the signs along the path and set the time for each, then whenever they pass a sign, it will produce a sense of accomplishment and bring them more motivation.

Questions:
1. How is SMART principle adopted in Huawei?
2. What can you learn from this?

【Study Questions】课后问题

1. What is the aim of setting goals?
2. What is the principle of setting SMART goals?
3. How to sort goals? What is strategic goal, tactic goal, or task goal?
4. How to test reality by defining urgency and importance?

Chapter 4   Audience Analysis
第4章   听众分析

Always know your audience. To make any type of communication as effective as possible, it is important that the communicator understands his or her audience. Audience analysis is a task that is often performed by successful communicator, which means assessing the interests, values, and goals of those people whom you want to influence to do something. The more you know your audience, the more effective communication you may achieve.

有效沟通需要建立在对听众理解的基础上。听众分析需要了解听众利益、价值、目标。越了解你的听众,你的沟通将会越有效。

In this chapter, you will:

- know the essentials in audience analysis;
- develop a strategy to target your audiences appropriately.

学习本章,你将会了解听众分析的要素,并建立合适的目标听众获取策略。

4.1   The Framework of Audience Analysis

一、听众分析框架

Audience analysis remains the most frequent challenge in business communication. By the time you've decided the goals you want to achieve, and why you are the person to do it, you probably need to start your audience analysis immediately. Table 4.1 shows the framework of conducting audience analysis.

听众分析是商务沟通中最具挑战的环节,当明确沟通对象(听众)后,应该即刻开始进行听众分析。

A proposal is much easier to be accepted

表格中的五个问题构成

Table 4.1　Audience Analysis Framework
表4.1　听众分析框架

#		
1	Who	• Who are my audiences?
2	Relationship	• What is my relationship to my audiences?
3	Attitude	• What are their likely attitudes toward my proposal?
4	Known Already	• How much do they already know?
5	Interests	• Is my proposal in their interests?

if careful audience analysis has been conducted in advance. For example, before applying a new policy in a company, the manager needs to identify who will be influenced (define target audiences), evaluate how much authority does he or she possess (the relationship between the communicator and the audience), assess the possible attitudes from different groups of audiences (are they positive, neutral, or hostile?), understand their knowledge (how much do they already know?), and judge whether this proposal fits their interests.

了听众分析的基础框架：明确沟通对象；分析听众关系；了解听众态度；了解他们的信息掌握程度；判断听众利益。

4.2　Define Your Audience

Defining audience seems simple. They are the people who you want to act or influence. However, if we look at "*audience*" from a bigger picture, you may find there are more group of audiences which play different roles that you need

二、明确沟通对象

明确沟通对象，不仅需要找出直接受到影响的听众，还需要在更大的视野里考虑听众包括哪些人群。

to pay attention to.

Primary audiences refer to key decision-makers and the people that have the authority to decide whether to accept your proposal and support you to carry out the project or not. Make sure they know all the information that you want them to know to look for their approval. When you, as a research group leader in R&D department, present a proposal for fund application to your boss, your boss, who has the resource and funds to support your project, is the primary audience in the communication.

Secondary audiences include those who will be affected by your project and who, over the long run, may have some influence on the decision-makers. For example, the sales manager disagrees with the budget plan on new product launching, from who's point of view, more money should be invested into channel distribution. This negative attitude probably could have influence on the decision-makers in some way.

In addition, there is yet another group of audience which is often ignored: the hidden audiences. Hidden audiences include those who may not be in the group you're addressing directly or on the receiving end of your E-mail, but who will have influence over whether the course of action you're recommending is adopted.

KOL is an acronym for Key Opinion Leader and can be defined as someone who's considered a connoisseur of a certain topic and whose opinions are

主要听众指关键的决策者或者对你提出的方案（沟通内容）拥有决定权的人。

次要听众受到方案的影响，或从长期看能够影响决策者。

潜在听众常常容易被忽视，虽然没有受到直接影响，但是潜在听众会在后续过程中以某种形式产生影响。

"意见领袖"随着移动社交媒体时代的发展而迅速崛起。社交媒体时代话语权一

respected by their public, thanks to their trajectory and the reputation they've built for themselves.

For that reason, KOLs have gained the status of experts and are recognized as referential people within their fields. Their achievements and skills are well-known, giving them an aura of authority.

In that respect, these profiles can be very valuable for carrying out actions, since they've already gained respect from their community and their opinions are always going to attract attention and be credible.

Today, the communication power of KOLs or other social media influencers, such as online celebrities, social media stars, content creators, is reinforced by the fast growing of social media (See Figure 4.1). Especially for people who have already made their name offline as key opinion leaders often become macro- or mega-influencers if they choose to operate social media accounts.

部分转移到以意见领袖以及网红、内容创造者等为代表的网民手中。

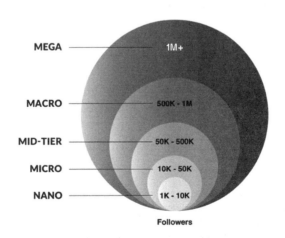

Figure 4.1　Influencer Tiers from Instagram
图 4.1　Instagram 粉丝量与影响力层级
Source: http://mediakix.com/influencer-tiers/#gs.GmeZP2bp

4.3 Relationship Analysis

After defining your audiences, it's of great importance to analyze the relationship between you and each group of them. When advocating a strong point of view to your audience, you need to adapt your presentation strategy to the realities of your relationship with them. Consider when a manager delivers an announcement to employees, or attends a negotiation meeting with buyers, the communication strategy might be different.

Mary Munter observed that, with the higher authority, and the lower audience involvement, the appropriate communication strategy would be tell, while with the lower authority, and the higher audience involvement, the appropriate communication strategy would be join. Most business communication falls somewhere in between (See Figure 4.2). The authority of the

三、听众关系分析

明确沟通对象后,需要进行听众关系分析,从而有针对性地制定沟通目标策略。例如,一位管理者向员工宣布一项决议或是与采购方进行谈判,不同的相互关系中,管理者的沟通策略将会是完全不同的。

玛丽·蒙特基于沟通者对内容的控制程度以及听众的参与程度提出沟通的目标策略可以分为告知、说服、征询、参与四种类型。

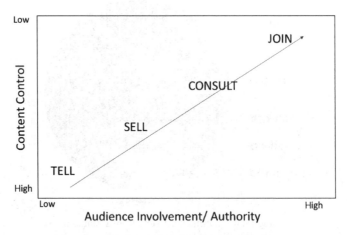

Figure 4.2　Audience Relationship Analysis Diagram
图 4.2　听众关系分析图示

communicator is derived from the content control power, which refers to not only the necessary position, title, or status, but also the information advantage that a communicator takes.

Tell: In this situation, the communicator is in complete command of the necessary authority and information. When a manager announces the budget of next fiscal year to the staff, the TELL approach would be adopted.

Sell: The sell approach is used when the communicator is in demand of the information, however, the audience retains the ultimate decision-making power. For example, a car dealer asks a customer to buy a new car.

Consult: This approach is often used when you are trying to build consensus for a given course of action. For example, you persuade colleagues to vote you as a group leader, or support your proposal on team-building day activities.

Join: Use the joint approach when your point of view is one among many. For example, you attend a cross-department panel meeting to discuss the impact of changing consumer behavior on product function design of your company.

In business context, taking proper approach to your audience leads the way to successful communication.

告知策略适用于沟通者完全掌握必要的权威和信息，并且听众对于沟通内容的参与程度很低的情况。

说服策略适用的情况是，沟通者掌握一定的信息，但最终的决策权掌握在听众手中。

当沟通者试图促使听众达成行动或共识时，可以考虑采取征询策略。

当沟通者的观点只是众多观点中的一种时，参与策略是比较合适的选择。

商务沟通中应根据情境恰当选择沟通策略。

4.4　Assess Audience Attitudes

四、评估听众态度

Since the audiences are mixed group of people, with different background, knowledge,

听众作为一个群体可能对沟通内容抱有肯定、否定

interest, and so on, the attitudes among them could be mixed too. The likely attitudes vary from positive, neutral to hostile. The communicator needs to apply different strategies and skills to reach audiences with different attitudes.

For positive audiences, who support the communicator, need to be motivated to take an action. Let them understand the importance and value of your proposal. Reinforce their favorable attitude by convincing them the benefits that will accrue and make their support worthwhile.

For neutral audiences, either they feel irrelevant to your proposal, or they are still in need of more information to determine. Try to provide neutral audiences with enough details and emphasize what they can benefit from it.

Negative audiences are hostile to your proposal. To communicate with hostile audiences, the communicator needs to take more efforts, do more analysis, and have more patience.

或者中立等不同的态度。针对持不同态度的听众应使用不同的沟通技巧。

对持肯定态度的听众应让他们相信自己的判断，并积极鼓励他们采取下一步行动。

对中立的听众提供足够的补充信息，强调其利益，鼓励其转化为积极的听众。

对待消极听众要付出更多的耐心和努力。可以试着去了解他们反对的原因，并从他们容易接受的问题着手，寻求解决问题的方法。

Tips and Advices

(1) Try to find out the reasons for the disagreement. For example, some audiences don't support your idea because they think they will be negatively influenced on their current interests, while some other audiences simply think the current proposal still has merits. These two reasons have totally different solutions.

(2) Convince them that although the communication seems not satisfying, it is worth to solve the problem somehow. Only when they consider the current situation and problems will they pay much attention to it.

(3) List the items that they may agree. It's easier for them to accept the idea

if they agree with some key factors. Thus, underline those points to make them well-known factors.

4.5 Ascertain Audience Knowledge

You will almost always want to ascertain your audience's levels of knowledge in the topic. What do they already know? You might have the experience of reading a newsletter full of clichés or listening to a presentation which is far beyond your knowledge. Communication like these experiences is likely to lose audiences' attention, or even turn neutral audiences into hostile ones.

Before communicating, consider how much do your audiences already know by asking yourself these questions:

- What background of this communication do they have? What familiar information should I summarize to lay the foundation for current communication?
- Will the content or language too hard for the audience to understand?
- What additional information need to be included for better understanding for my argument?

4.6 Arouse Audience Interests

What are the interests of your audience? The best way to sell ideas is to demonstrate that your

五、确定听众知识背景

听众分析还需要了解听众的认知程度。对于听众来说，听重复的内容和听完全不懂的内容一样令人沮丧。在这种情况下，听众的态度会向不好的方向转变。

在沟通前尝试了解一下听众都掌握哪些信息。根据听众的认知程度和认知能力我还需要补充哪些信息。我的内容和语言是否能被听众接受。

六、激发听众兴趣

听众对什么感兴趣？了解这一点将有助于抓住听众

argument is in the best interests of your audiences. What are the needs and expectation from your audience? Most importantly, knowing the interests of your audience will allow you to make sure that the information your audience needs most is presented in a way that is easy for them to locate and understand.

注意力。

Arousing the interests of your audience means identifying to both sides — the communicator side and the audience side — how they will benefit from being supportive. Table 4.2 shows the basic types of benefits and tips in communication.

激发听众兴趣可以通过强调听众利益实现。

Table 4.2　Types of Benefits and Tips in Communication
表4.2　听众利益与沟通要点

Contents	Tips in Communication
Tangible Benefits	Instead of just concentrating on the features you're trying to sell, show how those features will benefit the audience in a tangible way. Most business audiences respond well to bottom-line appeals (such as profit, results, gain outweighing cost, etc.). In addition to the bottom-line benefits, other tangible benefits may be more symbolic (such as offices, furnishings, or even just a pen or a mug)
Career/Task Benefits	Show how your audience will benefit in career path and personal development; you can also emphasize the appeals on the task itself (such as the opportunity and value)
Ego Benefits	Enhance the sense of self-value, accomplishment, and achievement with verbal and nonverbal communication
Group Benefits	Emphasize the benefits to the group developments, and how individuals will benefit from it
Consistency Benefits	Remind the audience of his/her record in history, and emphasize how important to keep consistency. Focus on benefits from personal credibility building through consistency in behavior

However, in business, benefits exist not only in positive contents. Sometimes, bad news could be beneficial to the audience in a way in the long-run. To communicate in this context, you may need to identify the negative influence on the audience currently, and determine what kind of positive influence could be generated if some actions are taken.

在消极信息的沟通中,你需要对听众分析对现状的负面影响,并说明如果采取怎样的行动将会取得的积极作用。

Example:
(1) To what extend would the audience been affected?
(2) Are there any consequences according to the background and situation of the audience?
(3) How to compensate the audience? Or what additional action should be taken to reduce the negative influences?

After positioning you as your audience's ally, you can identify the grounds of the audience's opposition appropriately, and find ways to soften the confliction and persuade the audience to take the attitude of facing the future.

当你和听众站在一个阵营里,你就可以识别出与听众存在的对立,并找到可以弱化冲突的方法,说服你的听众一起面向未来。

【Conclusion】本章小结

It is important that the communicator understands his or her audience. In this chapter, we discussed the methods of audience analysis. Defining your audience, making relationship analysis, assessing audience attitudes, ascertaining audience knowledge, and arousing audience interests are helpful steps to do audience analysis.

【Case Study】案例讨论

A Debate on 996 Work Culture in High-Tech Sector

> Alibaba Group founder and billionaire Jack Ma has defended the grueling overtime work culture at many of China's tech companies, calling it a "huge blessing" for young workers.
>
> The e-commerce magnate weighed into a debate about work-life balance and the overtime hours demanded by some companies as the sector slows after years of breakneck growth.

In a speech to Alibaba employees, in April 2019, Ma defended the industry's "996" work schedule, which refers to the 9 a.m. to 9 p.m. workday, six days a week.

"I personally think that being able to work 996 is a huge blessing," he said in remarks posted on the company's WeChat account.

"Many companies and many people don't have the opportunity to work 996," Ma said. "If you don't work 996 when you are young, when can you ever work 996?"

The issue has aroused an online debate and protests on some coding platforms, where workers have swapped examples of excessive overtime demands at some companies.

Ma, a former English teacher who co-founded Alibaba in 1999 and has become one of China's richest people, said he and early employees regularly worked long hours.

"In this world, everyone wants success, wants a nice life, wants to be respected," Ma said.

"Let me ask everyone, if you don't put out more time and energy than others, how can you achieve the success you want?"

Ma referred to the tech industry today where some people are without jobs, or working at companies in search of revenue or facing closure.

"Compared to them, up to this day, I still feel lucky, I don't regret (the days of working 12 hours), I would never change this part of me," he said.

"Creating a corporate culture of 'encouraged overtime' will not only not help a business' core competitiveness, it might inhibit and damage a company's ability to innovate," the *People's Daily* criticized 996 work culture on its MicroBlog.

The original speech delivered by Ma on an internal employee meeting:

About 996, now this is a very hot topic in China, many enterprises have this problem. Personally, I think it's a great blessing to be able to do 996. Many companies, many people has no chance to work 996. If you weren't 996 when you were young, when would you be 996? You haven't had 996 in your life. Do you think you're proud? In this world, every one of us hopes to succeed, to live a better life and to be respected. I would like to ask you, how can you achieve the success you want without the efforts and time to surpass others?

I don't want to say 996, so far, my working time is much longer than 996, even 12×12. There are many people in 996 in the world. There are many people who work 12 hours and 13 hours a day. There are many people who live harder, work harder and who are smarter than us. Not all people who do 996 can really do something valuable, meaningful and achievable.

So today, BAT companies in China have the chance to work 996. I think it's a good fortune for those of us. Think about people who don't have jobs, people who might close tomorrow, people who don't know where revenue comes from in the next quarter, people who worked so hard on an App that rejected by the market... Compared with them, to this day, I still feel that I am very lucky, I do not regret 12×12, I never regret this.

…

Also, what kind of company is Alibaba? Alibaba "let the world have no difficulty in doing business", this is our mission. I don't deny that our company is demanding. We have not told you that the company is very comfortable. "Let the world have no difficulty in doing business" is a tough job, and we are practicing our mission.

Today we have so many resources, we have a huge mission, hoping that in the future the world have no difficulty in doing business. Everyone, every individual should fully devote into our mission. So we say, to join Ali, you have to be ready for 12 hours a day, otherwise what do you expected to gain from Ali? We don't lack people who would like to work eight hours per day comfortably. Today, it is not difficult to recruit employees willing to work 8 hours a day, to sit in a good office with good cafeteria in a famous company. Such people can be found all over the street.

But what do we need? Let's ask you what exactly you want to do when you come to this company. It's about changing yourself, helping others, and fulfilling your mission.

Ali worked overtime in early years, but what did we do? After 8 hours of work, we stayed in company to study. What we have done wrong today? Where should be improved? How should we learn from each other? Two or three hours after work were for study and training, not for literally "overtime work".

I hope Ali people love what you do. If you don't love it, even eight hours will be too long for you. If you love it, 12 hours won't be too long.

……

乡村教师代言人-马云
今天 11:35 来自 微博 weibo.com
再谈996：理性讨论比结论更重要，周末愉快！

前几天我在公司内部关于"996"的观点，引起热议，批评声也是源源不断，和我预期的一样。有人奉劝我不要卷入这样的"不正确"话题，不讨人喜欢，主动招骂，还展示了"资本家的獠牙面目"……是在自毁"形象"。

我看了很多网友的回应，特别是骂帖，很多人很失望是因为从我嘴里说出这些"不正确"的话。我很理解这些看法，其实我完全可以说一些"正确的话"。但今天的社会不缺正确的话，我们缺的是实话、真话、让人思考的话。面对年轻人就是面对未来，面对未来我们不能视而不见。

 人民日报
今天 11:57 来自 微博 weibo.com
【人民日报评论：崇尚奋斗，不等于强制996】人们对"美好生活"的诉求不再是温饱时期的拼命工作赚钱，而是需要有在工作之外获得更多价值，发现兴趣、陪伴家人、寻找意义。没有人不懂"不劳无获"的道理。但崇尚奋斗、崇尚劳动不等于强制加班，不能给反对996的员工贴上"混日子""不奋斗"的道德标签。 崇尚奋斗，不等于强制996 收起全文

Questions:

(1) What is the context of this debate?

(2) Who are Mr. Ma's audiences?

(3) What message did Mr. Ma want to convey?

(4) What are the attitudes of each group of audiences?

(5) Did Mr. Ma's speech arouse audiences' interests?

【Study Questions】课后问题

1. Why it is important to make audience analysis?
2. How to define your audience?
3. How to make relationship analysis with Mary Munter's diagram?
4. How to react to the supportive audience? Hostile audience? And neutral audience?
5. How to arouse audience interests?

Chapter 5　The Message: Designing Contents and Structures

第 5 章　沟通的信息：设计内容与结构

Point of view helps audiences understand the perspective of the communicator. A communicator must have a place to stand — a point of view — upon which to design the contents and shape the arguments.

In this chapter, you will understand:
- how to clarify point of view;
- how to design content ;
- and how to shape the arguments.

5.1　Clarifying Point of View

What's your point of view when you communicate? Point of view means the perspective from which you assess a situation and present your findings and recommendations to your audiences. You need to review all the information you can reach, both the positive opinions and negative ones from audiences. The point of view should be your top priority to message design. As Archimedes said, "Give me a lever and a place to stand, and I can move the world." Taking a clear point of view will benefit in many aspects in business communication with subordinates or superiors.

Being explicit about your point of view is important when communicate with subordinates.

听众通过沟通者的观点了解其立场。观点是形成沟通内容和结构的立足点。

学习本章，你将会掌握沟通内容设计中的三个关键方面：观点、内容和论证。

一、明确沟通观点

沟通观点指评估形势或是阐述观点的视角。你需要审视所有可获得的信息，赞同或反对的观点，理解听众的立场。在上下级沟通中，明确的观点对于有效沟通十分重要。

对下级沟通应有明确的观点，否则下属将会没有工

An employee who does not clearly understand the manager's point of view may feel confused, which is possibly resulting in wasted time, or stress on the job.

Establishing and conveying clear point of view to your subordinates would be helpful in putting you and them on the same page. If they run into problems, they can seek assistance and avoid costly mistakes.

Clear point of view does not simply mean to ask the subordinates to obey every word of the manager. Today's leadership needs to appreciate that the key to better performance is good communication. Encouraging communication promotes decision-thinking teams. Through delivering clear point of view, the manager is easier to receive feedbacks from the subordinates, and moves the situation closer to action.

Making clear point of view is equally important when communicating with superiors. Nothing is more frustrating to the manager than listening to or reading a report that is pointless. In most management situations, a well-argued proposal, based on a clear point of view and supported by strong data will greatly improve communication efficiency and effectiveness. It's a way to refine your communication skills and to open further learning opportunities and the possibility for career development.

In business communication, you may state your positions clearly, and focus on your points to carry out the related explanation. As your view may differ from others, it is necessary to briefly

作方向从而导致低效甚至错误的工作。

如果理解了上级的观点，下属在遇到问题和困难的时候可以及时获取帮助。

明确沟通观点并非意味着要求下属遵守上级的每一句话，相反上级应该通过双向沟通打造有决策思维的团队。只有有效传递观点，管理者才能准确了解下属的反馈。

与上级沟通时明确沟通观点也同样重要。管理者希望收到下属的报告观点明确、数据翔实，而不是言之无物。良好的沟通能力对于职业能力培养和职业生涯发展至关重要。

在商务环境中，你提出了沟通观点后需要对你的观点立场进行解释。当你的观点与其他观点存在冲突时，

summarize the advantages and disadvantages of other points of view. Then discuss how your points of view will benefit the whole project or company in the short and long run. During these steps, pay attention to the reaction of other participants to ensure they understand what you are talking about.

需要简要总结一下其他观点并说明你方案的价值。

5.2 Designing Message

二、设计沟通信息

What message should be delivered in communication? Content refers to the message in communication that convey your points of view through certain argument.

内容设计是指你想传递的信息。内容是观点的具体表达。

In business, you are supposed to modify your message in order to achieve better communication goals toward different audiences. For example, as a marketing manager, you think it's necessary to increase the price of product A. Therefore, your communication goal is to convince different audiences that to "increase the price of product A" is necessary.

在商务环境中，你需要根据不同的沟通对象调整沟通内容。

To your boss:

According to marketing analysis, increasing the price of product A by 10% will receive an increase in net profit by 3.5% annually.

To your customers:

Product A with higher price features 10 more powerful functions.

You need to do audience analysis before you design the contents in communication. With good understanding in audience attitudes, knowledge, interests, the message will be better designed to reach communication goals.

在听众分析的基础上，根据对听众态度、知识、兴趣等的理解，合理设计沟通内容以实现沟通目标。

5.3 Shaping Your Argument

Arguments based on logic can help to persuade others to buy your point of view. Various situations in your academic, professional, and personal life will require you to be able to make a logical argument. Arguments refer to the way of delivering messages in order to be convincing or persuasive in communication.

The following steps describe how to shape your argument in communication.

1. Find Reliable Sources

Find reliable sources that support your point of view. Books, papers, government or university websites, peer-reviewed journals, well-known news publications, or documentaries are good places to start.

You can also do much of your research online, but you'll need to be careful about whether the sites you're using are reliable. In general, social media posts, personal websites, and collaborative websites where anyone can make changes are not reliable sources to cite. These are, however, a good place to gain a basic understanding of a topic.

In addition, finding reliable sources that support the counterargument is equally important. Explore an opposing viewpoint so that you can anticipate the arguments someone else will make against your point of view. For example, if you argue for taxing drivers in order to reduce pollution, search the ways in which taxes can have a negative impact on society.

三、形成论点

基于逻辑的论据能够帮助你在沟通中有效地获得支持。

可参考以下步骤形成论点。

1. 寻找可靠的信息源

通过可靠的渠道收集你的信息。书籍、报纸、政府网站、期刊等都是可靠的信息源。

网络资源也是很好的渠道，但需要进行辨别，类似社交媒体、个人主页等可以用作理解一个主题但不能视作可靠的信息源。

此外，寻找那些支持与自己观点相反的信息也同样重要，这样你可以了解别人为何会持不同观点。

2. Choose the Logic of Argument: Deductive vs. Inductive

The logic of deductive or inductive is the path a communicator takes to reach a conclusion. Given good audience analysis, persuasive message design depends on the effective use of logic and evidence. Deductive logic moves from general to specific, while inductive logic moves from specific to general.

With deductive reasoning, you will start with a major premise (generalizations) with a minor premise (specifications) to reach a conclusion.

2. 选择辩论逻辑：演绎与归纳

沟通者采用演绎或归纳的逻辑以得出结论。演绎法逻辑是从一般到具体；归纳法逻辑是从具体到一般。

演绎法逻辑从一个大前提（一般的）开始，再到一个小前提（具体的），最后提出结论。

> **Example:**
> Major premise: We need more experienced employees.
> Minor premise: My proposal will improve our employees' working experience.
> Conclusion: Therefore, my proposal should be adopted.

With inductive reasoning, you will assemble all the evidence, and then seek out the simplest explanation or conclusion. In business, inductive argument often outlines a series of problems, then proposes a general solution.

在归纳法逻辑中，你会列举所有的证据，然后从中找出最简单的说明或结论。在商务情境中，归纳逻辑法常常罗列一系列现象，然后提出一个普遍的解决方法。

> **Example:**
> 62 percent of voters in a random sample of 400 registered voters said that they support the new policy on medical care. This supports with a probability of at least .95 the following conclusion: Between 57 percent and 67 percent of all registered voters support the new policy on medical care.

This kind of argument is often called an induction by enumeration. It is closely related to the technique of statistical estimation. By this reasoning, if the premises are true, the conclusion might be true, or not. Inductive reasoning is typically used in cases that require some prediction.

3. Check Validity and Soundness

Argument should be both valid and sound. A valid argument is one in which, if all premises are true, the conclusion must be true. Soundness refers to whether the premises are actually true.

> **Example:**
> *Males are better educated.*
> *Educated person are more easily be promoted in companies.*
> *Males are more easily be promoted in companies.*

If all premises were true, the conclusion would be true, so it is valid. But obviously males are not necessarily better educated, so the argument is not sound.

4. Avoid Logical Fallacies

Avoid the following logical fallacies in communication.

(1) Hasty generalizations.

There are claims made without enough evidence. Don't rush to judgement without having all the facts. Making assumptions about large groups of people will undermine your argument and potentially offend others.

的科学性，并可能冒犯他人。

> **Example:**
> All employees support the training policy in this company.

(2) Circular arguments.

When you restate an argument while in the process of trying to prove a claim, you are making circular arguments.

（2）循环论证。

循环论证是指在试图证明一个主张的过程中将其作为论点。

> **Example:**
> Incentive travel is an effective incentive method by motivating employees.

(3) Personal attacks or suspicious motives.

Don't attack a person's character rather than their arguments or positions on certain issues. A person's character is unrelated to the issue at hand, and it makes you look biased against that person.

（3）人身攻击或怀疑动机。

不要攻击别人的性格，而是要聚焦其论点或立场。一个人的性格与当前问题无关，这让你看起来对他有偏见。

> **Example:**
> Timmy's plan won't solve anything because he is bad tampered and his intention is selfish.
> This doesn't address anything about Timmy's plan or how it affects the issue; it only attacks him personally.

(4) Avoid red herring arguments.

This is when you try to divert attention from something and, in doing so, avoid the key issues you should be addressing.

（4）避免红鲱鱼争论（即转移主要话题）。

当你试图转移话题的时候，就偏离了你应该解决的关键问题。

Example:

We should protect the environment by increasing tax on car drivers. Think how much faster your commute will be if there are fewer cars on the road!

This doesn't have anything to do with the environmental impact of cars or the economic impact of taxes.

(5) Try not to make either/or arguments.

Either-or arguments constrain people's imagination by giving others a strong impression that there are only 2 choices. However, there are almost always more than 2 options when facing a problem, so don't assume yours is the only solution. In negotiation, BATNA (Best Alternative to Negotiated Agreement) always exist if you look at the whole picture from another way. Present a strong case for your argument rather than scaring others into thinking it's the only way.

（5）不做"或者……或者……"式论证。

这种论证方式容易给人只有两个选项的错觉进而限制了解决问题的可能性。在谈判中，如果拓展思路，"最佳替代方案"总是存在的。

Example:

You can either accept this offer or go bankruptcy.

5. Emphasize Strong Evidence

Arguments depend on evidence. In business, evidence could be presented in different formats.

5. 强调有力证据

论据取决于证据。在商业中，证据以不同形式呈现。

1. Facts and Figures 事实和数据

Statistics is usually one of the best pieces of evidence, which could be presented in tables, charts, decision trees, regression analysis, etc. Arguments from this common type of evidence stand on accuracy, but accuracy is not enough. Demonstrating the relevance to the situation is as important as well.

2. Common Knowledge 共识

People used to take advantage of common sense. Business people, like social or political groups, tend to associate with others of similar responsibilities, backgrounds, common values. This is an easy way to collect information, however, it could also be the source where biases derived from.

3. Anecdotal Evidence 例证

Examples can provide powerful support for your argument. When use anecdotal evidence, make sure that it is relevant to your audience, in order that they can make comparison and can digest.

4. Authority 权威

With the help of authority, the audiences tend to believe more. Some writers will invite the celebrity or experts in some aspects to write the preface for them. It's same in the argument. Quote the words from business tycoon or even the bosses in your company will make your argument more persuasive.

There is no strong principle on how to rank the evidence in communication. However, start with your strongest evidence is most frequently used. Begin with your most compelling piece of evidence in order to begin convincing others of your viewpoint as quickly as possible. From there, you can work your way down until you end with what you view as the weakest aspect of your argument. Alternatively, you might present your weakest point next, then finish with a slightly stronger piece of evidence.

沟通中并没有关于将论据排序的明确原则。然而通常沟通会从最有力的论据开始，以便尽快说服听众。接下来，再提供弱一些的论据；或者，也可以在强论据之后陈述最薄弱的论据，然后用一个稍强的证据来结束。

【Conclusion】本章小结

In this chapter, we discussed the important items in contents design. As a communicator, you need to make clear point of view. In business context, point of view is of great importance in conditions when a subordinate reporting to the superior, or a superior communicating with a subordinate. The content is the message to deliver, which need to be structured with appropriate logic in a persuasive way.

【Case Study】案例讨论

JD.com Refutes the Mass Layoff Rumor

China's e-commerce behemoth JD.com denied the "mass layoff" rumor on Tuesday (Nov. 27, 2018) and claimed it had reported the case to the police.

On Tuesday, rumors went viral on China's social media that JD.com was to reduce its staff by 10 percent and its finance affiliate JD Finance (which has recently been renamed as JD Digits) by 15 percent.

It was also rumored women who are unmarried and/or without children, as well as probational employees, will be released from their contracts first.

The latest response from JD.com refuted the rumors, both about the layoff itself and the supposed terms, saying they are "exaggerations and truth-twisting".

Normal staff turnover is a routine part of every company, and optimization based on employees' performances is also not uncommon. Each year, JD.com conducts performance evaluations for all personnel, grants incentives to outstanding employees and adjusts the positions for those whose performance does not meet relevant requirements, the group said in a statement.

1. Increased Focus on Artificial Intelligence

This is not the first time that rumors of a mass layoff at JD.com have sparked discussion on social media.

In May 2018, Liu Qiangdong, CEO and founder of JD.com, noted at the World Retail Congress held in Spain that JD.com would become an unmanned company operated wholly by artificial intelligence (AI) and robots, and within 10 years, its employees would be reduced by over 50 percent.

To silence the rumors, Liu claimed that the company is currently gaining enormous momentum in growth, so JD.com still needs plenty of employees. He hopes that one day "everyone can be freed from hefty workloads, and the delivery men can sit in the office and monitor hundreds of robots working in the distribution."

Judging from the enterprise's latest moves to focus on smart logistics and building unmanned warehouses, JD.com is indeed poised to beef up its software and hardware via AI.

2. JD.com's Newfound Focus on R&D

JD.com's financial report shows that the e-commerce giant has invested heavily in R&D.

In the first three quarters of this year, the group's technological investments amounted to 8.64 billion yuan, far exceeding last year's figure. Among them, in the third quarter, JD.com invested a total of 3.45 billion yuan in R&D — a year-on-year growth of 96 percent.

At present, in terms of software, over half of JD.com's sales and cargo management are carried out with AI technology. Its second-generation AI customer service agents are even able to accurately identify the emotions of callers.

(Adapted from: Chinadaily.com.cn, 2018-11-29)

Questions:
1. What is the context of this "layoff rumor"?
2. Can you draft a letter to public in the name of Mr. Liu with the information given in the case? What point of view should Mr. Liu take? What message should he convey? What logic and structure should he design in his argument?

【Study Questions】课后问题

1. How to make clear point of view in a business context?
2. In business, how to modify your message in order to achieve better communication goals toward different audiences?
3. How to make valid and sound argument?

Chapter 6 Communication Channels

第6章 沟通渠道

Communication channels are the means through which people in an organization communicate. Using an inappropriate channel for communication can lead to negative consequences, therefore conveying messages through appropriate channels is of great importance to achieve various communication goals. Complex messages require richer channels of communication that facilitate interaction to ensure clarity.

In this chapter, you will:
- understand the types of communication channel;
- learn to choose appropriate channels according to communication goals.

沟通渠道是指沟通进行的途径。渠道选择不当将会给沟通带来负面效果。沟通复杂信息需要对多种渠道综合运用。

学习本章，你将会了解不同的沟通渠道类型；根据不同沟通目标选择合适的沟通渠道。

6.1 Communication Channel Types

一、沟通渠道类型

Since most business communications involve a variety of audiences, feature different conditions and goals, different channels are required to convey various messages.

在商务沟通中需要根据听众特征、沟通情境和目标来确定合适的沟通渠道。

1. Individual Communication vs. Group Communication

1. 个体沟通与群体沟通

One-on-One or individual communication is one of the richest channels of communication

一对一沟通（或个体沟通）是组织中常使用的沟通

that can be used within an organization. The more personal of your communication channel, the more likely your message will reach your audiences.

It is one of the best channels to get immediate feedback from an individual and build individual relationship and rapport. It is also an effective channel to use for complex or emotionally charged messages, because it allows for interaction between speaker and recipients to clarify ambiguity. A communicator can evaluate whether his messages have been received by audiences on the spot. Also, the communicator can ask or answer follow-up questions to improve mutual understanding in communication.

Group communication is both a science and an art. In group communication, the communicator faces various audiences at a moment. There is no doubt that group communication is more efficient than individual communication in terms of message delivering speed, however, since audiences vary in knowledge, attitudes, interests, etc., it needs to be more cautious to make group communication effective. In business organizations, without positive flows of communication, misunderstandings can occur between groups, creating a fractious work environment. In group communication cases, although you won't always be able to talk personally with each member of your audiences, you can usually do so with key decision makers or those important primary audiences.

(1) Small group meetings.

In small group meetings, everyone has the

渠道。个体沟通能将信息最大可能传递给听众。

个体沟通有利于收集反馈并构建双方关系。在某些复杂性沟通或是情感沟通场合，沟通者可以通过个体沟通确保听众准确了解到沟通内容，最大限度避免误解。沟通者也可以通过个体沟通中的反馈和提问及时发现问题，提高沟通效果。

群体沟通不仅是一门科学更是一门艺术，由于沟通者同时面对多个听众进行沟通，沟通效率大大提高。然而，由于听众的多样性，如何确保沟通效果值得仔细应对。特别在企业组织中，缺乏有效的群体沟通必然会影响绩效。此外，在群体沟通中，沟通者虽然无法接触到每一位听众，但仍然可以与群体中的主要听众（如决策者）进行个体沟通。

（1）小群体会议。

小群体会议是对人数规

chance to share thoughts and debate together. It can boost the team cohesion and staff motivation. Some managers think small group meetings can be better than personal communication, because the extreme views may be counterbalanced by more moderate views.

(2) Large group meetings

In large group meetings, the attendees meet and exchange views, convey a message, open a debate or summarize the key issues. These also show the leader is willing to face the troops and communicate with them.

2. Broadcast Media Communications vs. Electronic Communications Channels

TV and radio fall within the traditional broadcast media communication channels, which are generally used when delivering message to a mass audience. When a message intended for a mass audience can be enhanced by being presented in a visual or auditory format, a broadcast channel should be used. Before the age of Internet, it is one of the most influential way for a company seeking to notify customers of a new product to advertise or do promotions using a broadcast channel.

Electronic communication channels encompass email, Internet, Intranet and social media platforms. These channels can be used for one-on-one, group or mass communication. It is a less personal method of communication but more efficient. Some within an organization may opt to use this channel versus a face-to-face channel to save time and effort. When using this channel, communicator

模相对较小的群体进行沟通的方式，通过群体讨论交流交换意见，激发团队凝聚力；可以借助群体的力量一定程度平衡个体的极端观点。

（2）大群体会议

沟通者面对大规模群体的沟通方式，用以表达观点，开展辩论或是总结核心问题。

2. 广播媒体通信与电子通信

广播电视作为传统媒体在大众传播方面曾发挥重要作用。特别是在互联网时代以前，广电媒体是企业品牌推广最有影响力的沟通渠道之一。

电子通信包括email、互联网、局域网和社交媒体平台。这类渠道可以用作个体、群体或大众沟通，因其节约时间、注重实效而在组织中得到广泛采用。在使用中应注意内容的准确性，以免引起误解。

must pay attention to craft messages with clarity and to avoid the misunderstanding.

Live Broadcast: It was born for travel expenses and regional differences. Managers can reach their colleagues, partners, suppliers and customers more often without leaving the office. As the technology has matured, the attendees can also make an online interaction with the speakers. It's an efficient way which help mangers save time, resources and money and improve the working productivity.

随着跨地区商务沟通需要的增加，在线实时通信应运而生，极大降低了企业的沟通成本。

3. Oral vs. Written Methods of Communication

3. 口头沟通与书面沟通

In oral communication, not only the contents, but also the voice will influence the communication effectiveness. Especially when communicating face-to-face, physical presence, facial expressions, and other body languages are important factors that help audiences interpret that message as the speaker intends.

在口头沟通中，沟通者要特别重视肢体语言，如仪态、语气、表情等，对于沟通效果具有重要作用。

Written communication should be used when a message that needs to be formally conveyed, or limited interaction is required with recipients. Policies, letters, memos, manuals, notices and announcements are all messages that work well for this channel. Recipients may follow up through an electronic or face-to-face channel if questions arise about a written message.

书面沟通是一种正式的沟通渠道，在不需要与听众进行互动的情境下，也可以使用书面沟通，常见的如政策、信件、备忘录操作手册、说明、通知等。听众在收到书面沟通渠道的信息后，可以进一步进行反馈。

6.2 Considerations and Skills on Media Choices

二、媒体选择技巧

Modern enterprises increasingly rely on

渠道选择对于有效沟通

information and communication technologies to support flexibility in the business communication process. Using different channels to reach various types of audiences is critical to achieve communication goals. Mastering the choice of media has significant implications for productivity and efficiency of both individuals and organizations. The following factors need to be considered when deciding what media to use to convey your messages.

1. Urgency and Efficiency

How soon should the message be received by audiences? The communicator must consider the urgency of the situation and try to find the most efficient way to convey messages. Especially in crisis communication situations, the most efficient way to deliver message is highly valued.

2. Importance and Adequacy

Importance indicates that the communication channel needs to be most likely to acknowledge the importance of key audiences. From this approach, individual communication or small group communication are better ways to deliver important massages to key decision-makers.

Adequacy refers to the universality of targeted recipients in communication. The communicator should choose a media channel that can cover as many as possible and as accurate as possible of his/her audiences.

3. Complexity

Different audiences need different levels

具有重要意义。在商务情境中，面对不同听众需要有多种渠道选择策略，以下因素值得被仔细考虑。

1. 紧迫性与效率性

沟通者在选择渠道时需要考虑情境的紧迫性和沟通渠道的效率。特别是在危机处理中，信息传递的效率是重要的考虑要素。

2. 重要性与充分性

重要性是指对关键听众合适的信息传递渠道。这一渠道有助于关键听众掌握信息，个体沟通或小群体沟通是对重要听众传递重要信息的好方式。

充分性是指渠道是否能够覆盖目标听众群体。

3. 复杂性

不同的听众需要掌握不

of information. Choose the media appropriate to the complexity of the message and the needs of the recipients. For example, when there is good news and bad news mixed together, the attitude varies among audiences. The audiences that have been negatively affected need more explanation and emotional consolation than the positively affected audiences. The communicator needs to recognize the complexity of situation and choose different communication channels accordingly.

4. Cost

Communication need time, energy, and money. Cost is an important factor to consider in choosing media. The cost of mass mailings is much higher than mass emails. Press conference takes up a great amount of executive cost on time, labor and money than sending messages on website.

5. Consistency

The message conveyed should be consistency. Make sure all members of the audience receive the consistent message.

6. Modulation

Large audiences contain subgroups that will be affected differently by your announcement. Make sure each receive a message tailored to its needs and interests while avoiding inconsistencies or appearance of double-dealing. This is not an easy job. Communicators need to put effort into

同层面的信息。特别是当好消息和坏消息并存时，听众的态度就会很复杂，受到负面影响的会需要更多的解释和情感安慰。沟通者需要认知到沟通情境中的复杂性，选择不同的渠道达到沟通目标。

4. 成本

沟通需要耗费时间、精力和金钱。沟通者在渠道选择上需要考虑成本要素，某种类型的渠道会比另一种成本更高。

5. 一致性

确保所有的听众听到的信息是一致的。

6. 调适性

根据听众的不同类型、态度，对沟通内容进行调整，适应不同听众的需求。

reducing the hostile attitude of the negatively affected audience. Be sure to emphasize on future benefits on organization and individuals.

7. Feedback

Before sending out the massage, especially a negative one, make sure that you have the feedback channels ready to deal with the consequences. Make sure a mechanism is in place to air and address questions and concerns.

8. Timeliness

Get the message out before rumors develop. Use official and formal communication channels to increase credibility.

In business, the above factors need to be considered simultaneously by measuring and balancing among each other. There is not probably the best way, but always a better way to convey messages. Successful communicators will consider, and choose among, all the available channels (or media) through which they can send their messages and receive feedback: writing, speaking, videotapes, meetings, training programs, focus groups, posters, letters, radio and television, social events, newsletters, faxes, videoconferencing, the grapevine, surveys, and formal suggestion programs. Developing and implementing a successful employee communication program requires the manager to communicate effectively with colleagues, superiors, subordinates, and a variety of external media.

7. 重视反馈

在发出信息前，特别是一个负面消息前，确保你已经建立了反馈渠道以应对可能出现的后果，并为后续反馈建立良好的渠道和机制。

8. 时效性

注重沟通的时效性，避免谣言传播的最好方法是建立官方、正式的沟通渠道增加可信度。

在商务情境中，成功的沟通者会在各种要素、各种渠道类型中权衡考虑，选择最合适的沟通渠道。

【Conclusion】本章小结

The learning goal of this chapter is to understand that choosing the right media will determine the effectiveness of communication. The features of different communication channels are described, and some tips and skills on media choices are discussed.

【Case Study】案例讨论

1. Use Social Media for Customer Relationship Management

Online customer interactions with brands grew 70% between 2013 and 2014. According to McKinsey, 30% of these people prefer a direct message over sitting on hold on a customer service line. This is understandable. After all, this is an on-demand world. Waiting around for someone to answer the phone is a thing of the past.

The question now is not how companies can use social media to resolve issues. It is how they can use social media to develop deeper relationships with their customers.

2. Why Go Social?

The most compelling reason to move your CRM to social media is because this is where your customers now live. It is the best place to get closer to customers because you can connect with them wherever they are. It is in this anywhere-anytime connection that the huge potential lies.

Because of this potential, there is also the opportunity for other positive things. Building greater relationships with your customers can increase your revenue. The more connected you are with your customers, the more loyal they will be to your brand.

Also, moving CRM online can help you cut costs and become more efficient. The combination of fast feedback and collaborative problem solving results in faster resolutions. This means that you and your customers can get back to business with less time and money wasted.

3. Managing Customer Expectations

If you're going to use social media as a way to reach customers, it is best to play by their rules.

The social sphere wants instant communication. Customers expect this of their friends and they will expect this from you. In fact, one in four social media users think that brands should reply to their messages online within the hour.

This is where many social media newbies go wrong. To use CRM on social media in a productive way, you need to equip yourself with the tools you need to solve problems in this manner.

This preparation is essential. Mismanaging these problems can damage your reputation rather than strengthen it. This is because it all happens in the public sphere. Mistakes can live on the Internet forever.

Your customers also expect you to produce quality content. They are more interested in looking at news and information than they are in promotions. Thus, you should construct a strategy that offers a balance between the two.

Above all, you should aim to keep your voice genuine and your content engaging. This helps assure your customers that they are interacting with real people and not faceless companies.

4. Three Ways to Use Social Media for CRM

There are three great ways to use social media when working with customers.

The first way is to use it for managing complaints. Social media is a good platform for complains. This is because it is easier to deal with detailed complaints in writing compared to working over the phone.

To deal with complaints, you should follow a two-step process. In step one, you need to respond to the public message posted by the customer. This is crucial because it allows other people to see that you do respond to these messages.

In step two, you move the conversation into the private sphere. The best thing to do is to try to resolve it via direct messaging on the platform. Only if the situation is too complicated should you ever move away from the social media network.

Social media in CRM does not need to be all about complaints. In fact, you should also use it positively. A good way to do this is to reward loyal customers. Customers who engage with your brand online are valuable to you and expend a lot of brain power in advocating your business. Thus, you can and should provide them with the rewards and incentives to continue doing so.

You can reward them online by liking or sharing their posts. However, do not skip the offline rewards. You can reach out to your favorite followers to collect their details to send them special gifts.

Finally, you can use social media to create more value in your products. There are opportunities online for you to both upsell and cross-sell your products.

Using social media for upselling is not about the sales pitch itself. It is about taking advantage of the right opportunities at the right time.

This is why it is important to keep up with what your customers are saying. You will then see these opportunities begin to come up organically. This provides you with a moment to swoop in, offering a valuable solution to those in need.

Your customers are already online. If you choose to meet them, you can use social media to build deeper relationships that benefit you both.

(Adapted from: Benny Coen, www.socialmediatoday.com)

Questions:
1. Please talk about the role that social media plays in today's CRM. Why use social media for CRM?
2. How to use social media for CRM?
3. Discuss the side effects of social media for CRM?

【Study Questions】课后问题

1. What are the basic types of communication channels? What features each type?
2. What factors need to be considered when choosing media?
3. Overall, what suggestion would you give to a communication on choosing communication channel?

Chapter 7　Feedbacks
第 7 章　反馈

The ability to give and receive feedback is a critical managerial skill that doesn't come easily. What are effective feedbacks? How to give and receive feedbacks? When done right, both giver and receiver are inspired to improve business results and leap to higher performance.

In this chapter, we will:
- talk about the features of effective feedbacks;
- learn the skills of giving and receiving feedbacks according to different situations and scenarios;
- use feedback techniques for building trust, deepening relationships and creating viable paths for growth.

7.1　Feedback Essentials

Giving and receiving effective feedbacks are essential skills of a strong leader. Not only does it create an inclusive, supportive environment of personal development and growth, but it can also have a significant impact on how your company grows. In the following, we give a glance at the features of effective feedbacks.

给予和接收反馈是重要的管理技能，"什么是有效的反馈？""怎样给予和接收有效的反馈？"掌握反馈技能有助于提高管理绩效。

在这一章节里，我们将会讨论有效反馈的几大特点，学习根据不同的场景和情况来给予和接收反馈，掌握有效反馈技术以增进信任和关系。

一、有效反馈的特征

有效反馈是构建领导力的重要技能，其不仅可以为团队成员的成长创造包容和支持的环境，同时还能对企业成长产生巨大影响。

1. Effective Feedback is Specific, Timely, Meaningful, and Candid

In a business context, "effective" means your feedback needs to be specific, timely, meaningful, and candid.

(1) Specific.

"Feedback should have a clear business focus." Effective feedback should specifically tie into larger overall goal instead of being generic.

(2) Timely.

Feedback should be offered as close as possible to the action in question; It makes no sense to say, five months after the fact, "You know, Tom, you did a terrific job developing that new product back in April." The window of being able to reflect on behavior and change it has passed.

(3) Goal-referenced.

Effective feedback requires that a person has a goal, take action to achieve the goal, and receives goal-related information about his or her actions. Good feedback gives meaningful and actionable suggestions of how to adjust a behavior or change course and adds additional context that might have been originally missed.

For example, " Lucas, I appreciate if constructive suggestions on improving measures are included in this report."

(4) Candid.

Giving feedback is difficult. It's all too easy to duck tough issues when they emerge, but it helps no one.

No matter what your response to a behavior

1. 有效反馈是具体、及时、有意义且坦诚的

反馈应具体、及时、有意义且坦诚。

（1）具体。

反馈应该有清晰的业务焦点，而非泛泛而论。

（2）及时。

反馈应该越及时越好，从而保证针对反馈改进的时效性。

（3）目标导向性。

沟通者应有一个目标，采取行动，并收获目标导向下的行动反馈。好的反馈会对如何修正某个行为给出有意义且可行的建议。

（4）坦诚。

反馈并非易事，回避问题往往于事无补。若非坦诚面对，则将失去团队的信任。

is, you need to be honest or else run the risk of losing the trust of your team.

2. Effective Feedback Is Goal-Oriented and Focuses on the Future

"Effective feedback requires that a person has a goal, takes action to achieve the goal, and receives goal-related information about his or her actions," explains author Grant Wiggin. "Information becomes feedback if, and only if, I am trying to cause something and the information tells me whether I am on track or need to change course."

It's this subtle difference of giving advice that is clearly actionable that separates effective from ineffective feedback. Your feedback needs to tie directly into the goals of the person you're speaking with.

In everyday life goals can be implicit — if your friend is asking for feedback on a draft of a book they're working on, the goal is clearly to write a good book — but in the workplace, you need to explicitly remind people the goal they're working towards and tailor your feedback to explain how they're going to hit that goal.

Effective feedback understands that you can't change any event that has already happened. Instead, you need to be focused solely on the future and how you can help someone to change course in the hope to get closer toward their final goal.

3. Effective Feedback Is About the Process, Not the Person

One of the worst things you can do when

2. 有效反馈是针对目标、面向未来的

有效的反馈意味着一个人有着明确的目标，采取了行动去实现这个目标，然后收到了与目标相关而有效的行动信息。

有效的反馈应具有可行性，因此需要把反馈建议和对方的目标相结合。

与生活中的反馈目标不同，在职场里，你需要明确地提出需要完成的目标，并且针对如何完成那个目标给予反馈。

有效反馈总是关注于将来而非过去。

3. 有效反馈针对的是进程，而非具体的人

对事不对人：永远不要

providing effective feedback is let your emotions come into play. Effective feedback shouldn't be about the person, but about the action. As author Leo Babauta explains, "Never criticize the person. Always criticize the actions. And when you're making suggestions, make suggestions about actions, not about the person."

去批评个人，而是应该批评行为。当你给出建议的时候，也应该针对某种行为而非某个人。

> **Example:**
> Instead of saying "The presentation was too long and boring," better feedback would be
> "Instead of 2 or 3 examples on each slide, which distracts from the main message, limit yourself to 1 example per slide. This way, the presentation is more succinct and impactful and we'll be able to reduce it from 20 minutes to 15."

However, remember to always keep your feedback meaningful. Praising effort is another easy trap to fall into. You may think you're making things better by putting a positive spin on the situation, but, according to social psychologist Heidi Grant Halvorson, complementing effort after a failure not only makes people feel stupid, but also leaves them feeling incapable of reaching their goal.

反馈应是有意义的。积极的赞美同样也不利于有效反馈。

Keep it action-oriented. Keep it informational. And most of all, keep it about the process and what they have the power to change.

有效反馈是行动导向的，具备相当的信息量，应针对事件的进程以及如何去改进。

4. Effective Feedbacks Doesn't Assume It's Right

4. 有效的反馈不会假设自己总是对的

Difficult feedback is rarely about getting the facts right. It's about conflicting views, feelings, and values. Reasonable people differ about all

艰难的反馈很少是关于事实的梳理。

these things.

To get someone to truly change their behaviors, they need to respect what you're saying and trust that you have their best interests at heart. This all starts with a willingness to hear them out.

After you've given your feedbacks, ask them questions that show you're open to understanding what happened and want to nurture a supportive environment, including:

(1) How do you see the situation?
(2) How might you do things differently next time?
(3) What do you think worked, and what could have gone better?

The more an individual thinks about improving his or her performance, the more committed he or she is to making it happen.

7.2 Giving Effective Feedbacks

Now that we've established the requirements and features of effective feedbacks, it is about time that we move on to the giving and receiving of effective feedback, as they are essential among the skills of management. In reality, there are different settings and scenarios for giving and receiving feedbacks, but there are also general considerations for almost every case and scenario. Before we venture into the different scenarios, let's talk about the general considerations for giving effective feedbacks first.

要使别人真正改变自己的行为，应该耐心听取他们的想法，让其感受到反馈的良好意愿。

在给出反馈后，不妨向接收你反馈的人询问一些问题，以显示你愿意去理解之前发生的情况，并且乐于形成一种支持的环境。

一个人对于提高自己工作表现思考得越多，其越能够实现工作表现的提升。

二、提出有效反馈

鉴于我们已经讨论了有效反馈的要求和特征，那么接下来就让我们讨论如何给予有效反馈。

1. General Considerations for Giving Feedbacks

As a matter of fact, several key factors determine the effectiveness of most managerial feedbacks, and when you provide feedbacks to your superiors, peers and subordinates, please keep the following four factors in mind:

(1) Timing: is it the right time?

As we have discussed before, effective feedback is timely, because delayed feedback rarely works, and sometimes it would also be a problem if feedback comes too soon. For example, if a presentation has clearly not gone well, the communicator may need time to relieve his sadness before he can hear suggestions for improvement. The most timely feedback is a regular flow while a project is underway, and whenever you are about to give someone feedbacks, take some time to think about your timing, and ask yourself if this is the best time to give your feedbacks.

(2) Objectivity: is your feedback void of personal bias and sentiments?

Although absolute objectivity is impossible, and sometimes even undesirable, it is safe to say that objectivity is still a desired quality in feedback, because even though your judgements can inevitably have a subjective element, you still need concrete support to substantiate your judgement. For example, were projects completed on time? Were goals met? And did a communication have the

1. 给予反馈的总体考虑

虽然如何给予反馈视不同的场合和情况有着不同的选择和方式，但是有一些总体原则。

（1）反馈的时机性：反馈的时机正确吗？

虽然反馈的及时性很重要，但合理掌握反馈的时机同样重要。试想，当一位报告人做了一场失败的演讲而心情难过时，应该及时给予他演讲的改进意见还是先安抚他的心情？

（2）客观性：反馈是否避免了主观偏见？

绝对的客观反馈不仅是不可能的，有些时候甚至也是不可取的。但即便如此，仍需要在反馈当中尽量做到客观准确，用具体的事例和论据去支撑反馈的观点。如果没有论据支撑而只有主观感受，反馈意见也很难有效或是有说服力。

desired effect? Without such specifics, your feedback would appear to be too subjective or vague, therefore lacking in effectiveness and persuasiveness.

(3) Empowerment: focus on the things that could be changed.

Feedbacks must focus on things that the recipient has the power to change, whether he/she be a boss or an employee that's been slacking off. People are more likely to modify their behavior to accomplish the goals if you've given them the tools to do the job. For example, if you are giving feedbacks to the boss in the hope to win his/her approval for a project, then you'd better provide him with the information to make your case.

(4) Trust: two-way of exchange.

Although we sometimes learn valuable lessons from our adversaries, feedback is more readily accepted when it comes from a trusted source. A foundation for trust cannot be established in a one-way exchange; rather, it is a two-way exchange that requires mutual trust and respect. The best tool for building trust is praise and acknowledgement, because if you've recognized people's accomplishments, then they are more likely to heed you when you give out corrective feedbacks.

2. Giving Constructive and Corrective Feedbacks

Now that we've established the ground rules for giving effective feedbacks, there are also specific situations that need to be taken

（3）赋权：关注那些能够被改变的事情。

反馈应聚焦反馈接收人有能力作出改变的地方。如果希望人们改变自己的行为来达成某个目标，就需要为其提供具体工具或措施。

（4）信任：反馈的基础是双向的。

虽然有的时候我们会从对手那里学习到一些有价值的经验，但是就反馈来说，来自我们信任的渠道的反馈总是更容易被接受。信任的基础来自互信互敬的双向交流。

2. 给出建设性和纠正性的反馈

除了以上普适性的准则，在反馈时还应综合考虑，你将要给出的反馈是建设性的

into consideration while giving feedbacks. For example, is your feedback more constructive or more corrective?

When giving constructive feedbacks, praise and recognition are the most frequently used methods, as they suggest that the other party's performance is appreciated and corresponds to expectation, therefore reinforces the desired behavior.

On the other hand, if you are giving corrective feedbacks, your methods need to be subtler, as they can sound accusing or derogatory if not taken well. In this case, you may as well try "the hamburger method", that is: you start by giving a positive, encouraging statement, and follow that with corrective suggestions or constructive criticism, and then some more positive words. The positive statements are like the "bread" of the hamburger and the criticism is the "filling" and real stuff. Just make sure that your criticism or suggestions are well-grounded and good-intended, as we have discussed in the opening part of this chapter.

3. Giving Feedbacks to Superior, Peer and Subordinates

Giving feedbacks to the person who signs your paycheck or supervises your work can be intimidating. But if you have to or if you choose to do so, the above-discussed rules and suggestions still stand.

In addition, you may want to assess the

还是修正性的？

当给出建设性反馈时，最常见的方法是进行称赞和认可，从而强化你从对方身上希望看到的品质和表现。

修正性反馈需要更加迂回，以免对方将反馈视为责备或贬损。

"汉堡包反馈法"常用于修正性反馈，在一开始就给出一些正面的鼓励性的反馈，然后提出修正性意见或批评，最后再补充一些积极正面的反馈——就像汉堡包的构成一样。

3. 针对上级、平级和下级给予反馈

虽然给上级做反馈有时很艰难，但同样应遵守上述原则。

此外，在提出反馈之前

situation before giving your feedbacks, as most managers welcome feedbacks that are intended to increase workplace efficiency or productivity, so your intentions should be focused on some benefit to the business, not to yourself.

You may frame your feedbacks in terms of your own personal observations, but you may also try to see things from your manager's perspective. If you have a problem with the way they're doing something, figure out why they've chosen to use that method and how it benefits them. Make sure it's more than just a personal pet peeve of yours.

In contrast, when giving feedbacks to your peers or subordinates, aside from the above guidelines and principles, you may want to evaluated strengths and weaknesses in light of agreed-upon goals and objectives, as workers' performances cannot be usefully evaluated unless the specific tasks and overall objectives they were charged with are reasonably clear. Also, you may want to be specific and strive for a matter-of-fact tone when you send out your message, as you don't want to sound obsequious, coy, apologetic or condescending. And most importantly, you need to practice what you preach, because it is hard to complain about another's interpersonal skills if your own are somewhat lacking, or to point our missed deadlines if you are known to procrastinate.

7.3 Receiving Feedbacks

Aside from giving feedbacks, we sometimes

应进行充分评估。上司对于提高管理效率的反馈都是欢迎的，反馈应该聚焦于如何让公司受益，而非个人。

试着分别从自己和管理者的角度来看问题。特别是当对某种管理方式有意见，在提出意见前不妨尝试去理解这种管理方式的采用原因和带来的益处。

对平级或下级给出反馈时，除了前面讨论过的方法，还应基于共识的目标评估优劣势。

此外，反馈的措辞也应该尽量具体并采取实事求是的语气。

最重要的是，行胜于言，如果是你自己也做不到的事情，即便你讲了出来也很难令人信服。

三、接收反馈

接收反馈包含收集反馈、

also need to receive feedbacks from others at work. As recipients of feedbacks, how to handle the feedback that we receive is equally important, as communication is a two-way process. This process may involve soliciting feedbacks, receiving feedbacks and evaluating feedbacks.

1. Soliciting Feedbacks

When you need feedbacks, how can you get them?

In fact, in every step and stage of a project, feedbacks are needed to ensure the project is on the right course. When you need feedbacks from others, the best and most often used method is to ask directly, but it can vary according to the size and variety of your audience.

If you are trying to persuade one person, you may go ask him/her or feel out his/her views ahead of time in informal conversations; if you are addressing a small group, you may test your ideas against representative members whom you trust; with large audiences such as all the employees of a corporation or the general public, you may need to conduct focus groups or to commission a professional survey.

But no matter how you do it, you may insist that they prioritize helpfulness and focus on what you can be doing in the future. Giving honest feedback can be intimidating; understand this before you approach someone for feedback. Make them feel at ease by letting them know you appreciate honesty from them more than an

听取反馈，以及评估反馈三个阶段。

1. 收集反馈

如何获取反馈？

在项目进展的各个阶段，都需要听取反馈以确保其顺利进行。除了直接询问他人的反馈意见，收集反馈的方式方法因听众的规模和类别而有所不同。

针对个人的时候，可以开展非正式的询问；而针对群体的时候，则可能需要从中选取你信得过的几个代表作为听取反馈的对象，或是开展焦点小组讨论甚至进行一次专业的调研。

无论采取哪种具体方式，在收集反馈的时候都应强调他们的反馈将会带来的帮助，并尽可能地打消对方的顾虑，让对方感觉到自己能够畅所欲言。

attempt at not hurting your feelings.

Also, you can ask for feedbacks on a regular base and prepare a list of specific points that need feedbacks. This way, the people that you ask will know better what this is about and what you want to know from them. In the meantime, you can also bring some timely, important information concerning projects you're working on to the table. This will make the interaction more of a conversation, while also making you come across as more helpful.

2. Receiving Feedbacks

After feedbacks soliciting, it is time that you hear out the messages been sent to you, and that sometimes can be even harder than telling, as the feedbacks one receive can rarely be completely positive. In whatever case, make sure that you don't get defensive and always listen to what they have to say, as most of us must make a conscious effort to receive criticism constructively.

Even if you're told something, whether positive or negative, that you don't agree with, avoid the urge to start a debate, because the best way to kill any chance of regularly getting constructive feedback is to interrupt the person to defend yourself. Either they'll feel like they're wasting their time and get discouraged, or they'll try to be polite and stop giving feedback.

Instead, you should strive to understand your respondent's goals. Whether you're listening to bosses or subordinates, you won't fully understand

此外，还可以定期或经常性地收集反馈意见，并为那些需要反馈意见的问题列一份清单，以便让你的听众能够更充分地了解你的问题和诉求。

2. 听取反馈

在收集到反馈后，如何听取反馈至关重要，因为不是所有反馈都是积极正面的。这个时候，你需要做的是有意识地以建设性而非防御性的态度去接收批评。

当对反馈存在异议时，也不要开展争论，而是应该让对方把话说完，否则他们要么会不想再说下去，要么会出于礼貌或压力而刻意隐瞒真实想法，从而丧失有效反馈的意义。

应尽力理解对方的意图。不论对方是上级还是下属，都应该先搁置自己的目标而

them unless you temporarily set aside your own goals and focus on what they want to express. Anyone who has devoted time and thought to review your work deserve to be heard, and you can't benefit from responses that you haven't understand.

3. Evaluating Feedbacks

Evaluating feedbacks means evaluating your sources. Not all feedbacks are worthy of further consideration once we've actively listened to what the person giving the feedbacks has to say. Each circumstance is different and you must assess the value of the feedbacks and decide if, how, and when to follow up on it. Are the respondents reliable? Do they have your best interests at heart, or are they pursuing their own agenda?

People giving you feedbacks on a specific performance-period, communication or proposal may respond in three ways:
- They can report their experiences as workmates, readers or listeners.
- They can identify strengths and weaknesses
- They can suggest improvements in your analysis or plan of action.

When receive such feedbacks, you should look for misunderstanding first. That is: are your own words or actions misinterpreted? If so, you probably need to modify your communication strategy.

Next, you should look for valid arguments against your own position. Has your respondent

聆听反馈意见。如果不能充分理解对方的意图，那么将很难从反馈当中受益。

3. 评估反馈

对反馈意见进行评估意味着对意见的来源进行评估。在听取了反馈之后，并非所有的意见都值得完全遵照或吸收。例如：信息来源可靠吗？提供反馈的人是否有个人利益诉求？

就特定的绩效、沟通或提案提供反馈。

报告自己作为同事、读者或听众的体验。
指出优势和劣势。
指出需改进的部分。

当收到以上类型反馈时，首先应该检查自己是否被误解。如果有，应及时调整沟通策略。

其次，应检查反馈中是否有论据充分的修正性意见，

discovered real flaws? If so, maybe you need to go back and take a thorough review of your work or proposal.

Thirdly, you should look for unforeseen grounds of opposition, as these feedbacks can help you reshape your message or performance.

Last but not least, value those suggestions on how you can perform or communicate better, and follow up through words, actions, and/or modified behaviors.

反映了真实的问题和缺陷；如有则改进并弥补缺陷。

再次，应检查反馈中是否包含未曾预见的反对立场。

最后，对于那些能够提高自己表现的反馈意见，应表达重视和感谢。

【Conclusion】本章小结

Giving and receiving effective feedbacks are essential skills in managerial context. In this chapter, we discussed the skills of giving and receiving feedbacks according to different situations and scenarios. The students are encouraged to understand and practice feedback techniques for building trust, deepening relationships and creating viable paths for growth.

【Study Questions】课后问题

1. What are the features of effective feedbacks?
2. How to give effective feedbacks?
3. What need to be paid attention to when receiving feedbacks?

Chapter 8　Put It Together: Panoramic Analysis on Communication Strategy

第 8 章　管理沟通策略之全景分析

Management communication is different from other kinds of communication, because in business setting, the message is useful only if you achieve your desired outcome. Therefore, considering communication from the overall basic elements, which including communicator, audience, message, feedbacks, channel, goal and context, will help you make a successful communication.

In this chapter, you will:
- learn to put the 7 basic communication elements together to analyze communication scenarios;
- understand 5 basic management communication strategies, which are communicator strategy, audience strategy, message strategy, channel strategy, and cultural strategy.

这一章我们综合运用管理沟通七大基本要素——沟通者、听众、信息、反馈、渠道、目标、情境——对管理沟通策略进行全景分析。

学完本章后，你将能综合运用七大要素对沟通情境进行分析；了解管理沟通的五大基本策略，包括演讲者策略、听众策略、信息策略、渠道策略、文化策略。

8.1　Framework on Panoramic Analysis

1. Review on Basic Elements of Management Communication

一、管理沟通全景分析

1. 管理沟通基础要素的回顾

In previous chapters, 7 essential elements in communication are discussed respectively. Communication is a united and integrated process,

沟通是一个将各要素整合的过程，在本章我们将把此前各章的沟通要素整合起

in this chapter, we will put the elements together and make panoramic analysis.

Before we start, we need to review once again the basic 7 elements in management communication — communicator, audience, message, feedbacks, channel (media), goal, context. You may refer to Figure 1.2 in Chapter 1 and make a review of each element.

来进行分析。

在开始本章内容前，有必要将前七章的内容进行系统复习。请大家结合图1.2七大沟通要素图，回顾每个要素的要点。下面的问题可以帮助你进行复习。

Review

1. Source

How to be a reliable source? What are the fundamental features of a successful communicator?

2. Goals

What is the principle of setting goals? How to sort goals?

3. Audience

Who are your audiences? What is your relationship to your audience? What is the attitude of your audience? What does your audience already know? What is the interest of your audience?

4. Message

How to make your point of view? How to design your message and shape your argument?

5. Channel (media)

What are the differences between different types of communication channel?

6. Feedbacks

How to give and receive feedbacks effectively?

7. Context

Consider urgency-importance and reality text on context when you do analysis on communication elements as a big picture.

2. Communication Factor Decomposition Diagram

Any business case includes a complex process — the communicator, audience, media, message, feedbacks, and goals overlap. Each scene happens in different scenarios (contexts). Communication Factors Decomposition Diagram is instructed to help us sort out complex cases clearly, in the hope that you can find the impact factors of achieving communication goals in each scenario.

With the following reading material, we will discuss the method to instruct a communication factor decomposition diagram.

2. 沟通要素分解表

商务沟通是复杂的过程——七大要素相互重叠,并且发生的情境也不一样。**沟通要素分解表**将会帮助我们把复杂的案例梳理清晰,从而你可以发现每一个场景下达到沟通目标的影响要素。

我们将借助以下阅读资料说明沟通要素分解表的编制方法。

Reading

Beijing Woman Finds Feathers in MD's Chicken Wings

Most recently, Ms. Zhou, a woman in Beijing said her daughter took a bite of the chicken wings from MD Restaurant and found feathers in her meal.

The sight made the girl nauseous. But by then, she had already eaten three chicken wings.

They were part of a takeaway meal that was purchased on the evening of April 21, 2019.

While she did not show signs of illness, the incident did affect the girl's appetite.

Her mum went to the restaurant to alert them of her discovery but declined the compensation offered by MD Restaurant. Complaints are proposed to the Food and Drug Administration.

"The feathers were still attached to the chicken wing. We have questions about how the restaurant handles food safety," she told Chinese media in an interview.

The woman then lodged a report with the State Food and Drug Administration.

Many Weibo users left messages expressing disgust and shock. Some Weibo users, however, are casting doubts on the incident, saying that the feathers would not look like the ones in the photos if they had gone through the deep fryer. Another user suggested that it could be a case of food sabotage by a restaurant worker.

The restaurant apologized to the customer on April 23, and said that it is now looking into the case and it will improve restaurant management.

The next day, MD Restaurant posted on Weibo, "The restaurant attaches great importance to this matter and has actively launched an investigation. We sincerely apologize for the trouble caused to customers by the failure of restaurants to detect product defects in time. We will strengthen restaurant management to provide better service for consumers."

(Adapted from: Sohu News, 2019-4-25)

This reading case provides a classic scenario of business communication, because it presents the sort of raw evidence any manager is likely to encounter. It encourages students to pull together the critical elements they've been discussing in the previous chapters. We will discuss from the perspective of MD's PR department. In Table 8.1, an example of Communication Factors Decomposition Diagram is developed.

这个案例提供了非常经典的管理沟通分析素材，学生可尝试将前7章的内容整合起来，将表8.1所示的沟通要素分解表补充完整，建立一个系统分析的框架。

Table 8.1　Communication Factor Decomposition Diagram
表 8.1　沟通要素分解表

Contexts	Goals	Audiences	Messages	Media	Feedbacks
Food safety concerns	Gain victim understanding; Express sincerity in fixing problems	Ms. Zhou; (hostile attitude)	Understand your feeling; Deeply regret the incident; take Responsibility; Investigate the incident.	Individual communication Face-to-face	Give feedbacks on investigation
MD is strict with management control system	Strengthen restaurant management	Restaurant staff	Investigation on food producing safety control; Policy on service procedure; Punishment on staff responsible	Group communication; Individual communication on key staff	Interaction with staffs
...	...	Public	...	...	...
...	...	Government Administration	...	...	...
...	...	...	...	...	...

Since we discuss this case from the perspective of MD Restaurant, the communicator is the company manager or department manager supposedly. The students could finish the diagram and analyze each element of a communication situation. In addition, the students could practice to analyze from the consumer's perspective and other perspectives.

表8.1是基于公司视角作出的沟通要素分解，在此基础上，学生可尝试从不同视角制作沟通要素分解表。

8.2　Panoramic Analysis on Communication Strategies

二、沟通全景分析的五大策略

After reviewing the basic elements in

本章将提出管理沟通的

communication, we will put them together and make panoramic analysis, which is to look at management communication strategies in a big picture. Within the framework of panoramic analysis, five management strategies are discussed respectively in this chapter, including communicator strategy, audience strategy, message strategy, channel strategy, and cultural strategy (See Figure 8.1).

全景分析——五大沟通策略，即沟通者策略，听众策略，信息策略，渠道策略和文化策略。

将五大沟通策略整合运用有助于提高沟通效果。

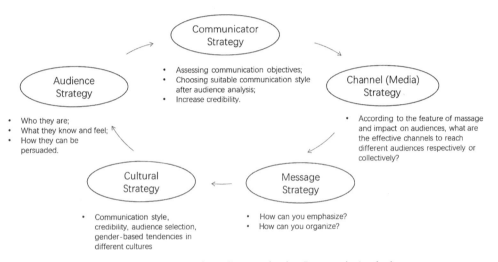

Figure 8.1　Framework on Communication Panoramic Analysis
图 8.1　沟通全景分析框架图示

1. Communicator Strategy

The communicator is the message sender, and is the key of successful communication. In order to make this process smooth, the communicator need to consider: What is your objective? What style of communication do you choose? How to build up your credibility?

(1) Setting appropriate communication objectives.

As a communicator, it's important to consider

1. 沟通者策略

沟通者即信息发送者。需要明确：沟通目标是什么？用什么方式？我是合适的沟通发起者吗？

（1）制定合适的沟通目标。

沟通者在发起沟通前应

the objectives before communication starts. Effective strategic communicators are those who receive their desired response or outcome. However, the objectives could be unclear, or could be too general. Therefore, the communicators need to make analysis on communication objectives, then set the objectives in an order, often from the general to the specific (See Table 8.2).

The communicators may set the general objective (strategy), the action objective (tactics), and the communication objective (tasks), then planning communication process from the specific objectives.

General objective (goal): It is the broad overall goal toward which each separate communication will aim.

Action objective (goal): Break down the general objective into a consciously planned series of action outcomes that lead toward the general objective. The action objective is a setting of specific, measurable, and time-oriented steps.

Communication objective (goal): The communication objective is even more specific. It is focused on the result you hope to achieve from a single communication effort. For example, through a specific effort, such as a report, an email, a presentation, what message you would like your audience to achieve and then lead to an act.

认真思考沟通目标。然而沟通目标有时可能是不明晰的，有时可能很大，因此，沟通者要分析沟通目标，然后对沟通目标细分，使其从一般到具体。

沟通者建立清晰明确的总体目标、行动目标、沟通目标，然后从具体的沟通目标开始谋划沟通。

总体目标是综合目的，是沟通者所希望实现目标的概况与阐述。

行动目标是指向总体目标的具体的、可度量的并有时限的步骤。

沟通目标更具体，以行动目标为基础，描述了希望听众作出的反应。例如通过具体的一个报告、一封信或邮件、一次交谈、一个电话等，你想让你的沟通对象了解什么信息，进而采取行动。

Table 8.2   Examples of Objectives
表 8.2   制定目标示例

General Goal	Action Goal	Communication Goal
Increase the number of customers	Contract with 30 customers per month	As a result of this visiting, the client will sign the contract
Achieving recruitment objectives	Hire 5 salesmen by the end of next month	After this meeting, a recruiting plan will be developed by HR department; After this interview, 8 candidates will be recommended into next round of interview with sales manager
Maintain market share of a product	Making a new marketing plan	After this presentation, the new marketing plan will be approved by CEO; After this meeting, our sales team will understand this new plan

(2) Choosing suitable communication style after audience analysis.

After defining communication objectives, the communicator needs to make analysis on audience and choose a suitable communication style to reach that objective. When advocating a strong point of view to audience members, you must adapt your presentation strategy to the realities of your relationship with them. As you telling them or asking them to do something? Most business communication falls somewhere in between. You take one approach when delivering a proposal to a committee of superiors and another when assigning a task to an assistant.

In *Guide to Managerial Communication*, Mary Munter offers a useful model of how to determine your approach to your audience. She

（2）基于听众分析选择适合的沟通形式。

当沟通者确定沟通目标后，就要基于听众分析选择合适的沟通形式传达信息，以使你的沟通战略符合你们之间的关系现状。

你是告知还是请求他们做什么事？许多管理与商务情境处于两者之间，与上级和与下级的沟通形式应有所差异。

在《管理沟通指南》一书中，玛丽·蒙特根据沟通者对信息的控制程度和听众

categorized the communication styles into 4 approaches according to the communicator's content control and the audience involvement, which were tell, sell, consult, and join. The communicator needs to assess relationship to the audience and shaping suitable communication style. Message strategy will be developed to carry out the communication plan.

(3) Be a successful source: the function of "iron triangle".

"Iron Triangle" refers to the basic elements that a communicator should pay attention to, which are, good wills, you-attitude, credibility (See Figure 8.2).

的参与程度，将沟通形式分为告知、说服、征询、参与。

（3）成为优秀沟通者的"铁三角"定律。

"铁三角"指的是优秀沟通者的三个基本原则：良好意愿、换位思考、增加可信度。

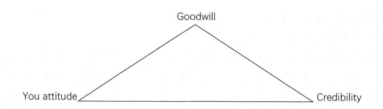

Figure 8.2　"Iron Triangle" in Communication
图 8.2　管理沟通"铁三角"

Another important aspect of communicator strategy involves your audience's perception of you, which includes trust, familiarity, and impression. Perception from audiences may have a huge influence on your choice of communication strategy.

According to social power theorists French, Raven and Kotter, there are five factors affecting your credibility: rank, goodwill, expertise, image and common ground. To enhance your credibility,

听众的看法和认识将会影响沟通策略制定，包括听众的信任度、熟悉程度以及好感度等。

影响沟通可信度的五因素包括社会层级、良好意愿、专业技能、外在形象和共同立场。应充分理解并运用五

you need to understand each of these factors, strengthen your initial credibility and increase your acquired credibility.

By "initial credibility", we mean your audience's perception of you before you even begin to communicate. It may stem from their perception of who you are, what you represent, or how you have related to them previously. In contrast, "acquired credibility" refers to your audience's perception of you as a result of what your write or say.

In order to achieve the desired result of communication, you can stress or remind your audience of the grounds for your initial credibility, and exhibit your good ideas or persuasive writing and speaking to earn acquired credibility. Also, you may associate yourself with a high-credibility person, acknowledge values you share with your audience, or use other techniques as listed on the following chart.

2. Audience Strategy

Peter Drucker mentioned that "communication takes place in the mind of the listeners, not of the speaker", which means that it is not enough to know what you want for the audience as the result of communication, but you also need to know where they stand right now, and that includes who they are, what they know, what they feel, and how they can be persuaded.

(1) Who are your audience?

This may sound like a simple question, but in

因素强化沟通者的初始可信度和后天可信度。

"初始可信度"是指沟通前听众对沟通者存有的看法。这些看法可能来自他们对你是谁，你代表着什么，以及你之前和他们发生过什么的感知；"后天可信度"指的是听众在沟通以后对你形成的认识。

为了达成沟通效果，沟通者应强化初始可信度的因素，通过联系和联结加强后天可信度。

2. 听众策略

有效沟通需要了解听众，包括他们是什么人，他们知道些什么，他们的感觉如何，以及他们可以如何被你劝说。

（1）你的听众是谁？

在实际的商务沟通中，

real-world business communication, the answers to this question may be very complex and subtle. It may include:

Primary audiences, i.e. the audiences who will actually receive your message directly. Primary audiences generally include key influencers, as usually one or more audience members have more control over the outcome of the communication, such as your client or customer, as they can make the decision whether to buy your product or not; also, some opinion leaders and the gatekeepers such as an assistant can also affect the final decisions, as they can either facilitate or impede your communication. All these people that have more influence on the outcome of communication can be labeled "key influencers".

Secondary audiences are the people who will receive your message indirectly (such as receiving a copy).

Hidden audiences include those who may not be in the group you're addressing or on the receiving end of your E-mail, but who will have influence over whether the course of action you're recommending is adopted.

All these audience types need to be taken into consideration while preparing your content of communication, and it is even better to prepare with different emphasis on the content for different groups, so as to make effective communication on all levels.

(2) What do they know and expect?

Before you decide what to tell your audience, perhaps you need to think about what they already

准确找到你的听众并非易事。

主要听众是那些将会直接接收到你的信息的听众，其往往包括富有影响力的关键性听众，也就是那些对沟通的结果有着更多控制权的少数听众。

次要听众，也就是那些能够间接接收到你的信息的人。

潜在听众常常容易被忽视，虽然没有受到直接影响，但是潜在听众会在后续过程中以某种形式产生影响。

在沟通前，所有听众的类型都应该被纳入考量，并有针对性地进行准备，以便关键信息得到有效的传播。

（2）听众已知和期待的信息是什么？

沟通前应了解听众背景，

know and what they expect to hear from you. You may take their age, education background, occupation, ethnic origin, gender and culture into consideration.

Empathize with the novices: assume your audience aren't the connoisseurs of your field, so take that background into consideration and remove the terminology and jargons in your message, or you can just simplify the information and focus on the ideas that are essential to your main point.

Deal with mixed background needs. In managerial communication, we usually find ourselves in face of a mixed audience. In these cases, you may want to aim your message toward the key decision makers in your audience while providing as much information to the rest audience as possible, such as handing out background materials beforehand.

(3) What do they feel?

Please keep in mind that the audience's emotional level is as important as their knowledge level. Therefore, aside from thinking about what they already know, you also need to think about how they feel, and the following questions could give you some hint in this regard.

What emotion do they feel right now? To answer this question, you will need to know about their current situation, and ask yourself about what emotions they might feel after hearing your message.

How interested are they in your message? If

分析哪些信息是听众已经知道的，哪些是他们所期望听到的。

照顾外行的感受，避免使用过于艰深的专业术语，宜使用简单的语言进行替换。

照顾背景各异的听众。在照顾不同的听众的同时（如为不熟悉背景情况的人提供背景资料等）着重考虑向听众当中的决策者传达你想表达的信息。

（3）听众的感觉如何？

听众的情绪水平和他们的知识水平一样重要。除了考虑他们知道什么，你还需要思考他们的感觉如何。

他们当下的情绪如何？沟通者需要了解听众当下的处境以及沟通后他们可能会有什么感觉。

他们对沟通内容有多大

their interest level is high, you can cut to the point without much time to arouse their interest. But if their interest level isn't as high as you expect, then you probably would want to adopt a consult/join style and ask them to participate, because one of the best ways to build support is to share control.

What is their probable bias, and is their bias positive or negative? If they have positive or neutral attitude toward your message, you can reinforce their attitude during communication to achieve your desired result. But if their attitude toward your message is negative, then you will need to employ some other techniques to make your communication smoother. For example, you can keep your request to the minimal or break it down to smaller requests, or you can propose a pilot program instead of a full program to begin with.

Is your desired action easy or hard for them? From the audience's perspective, is your desired result of communication an easy job? If it is not so easy, then you might want to break it down into the smallest possible requests, and make the action as easy as you can. But no matter easy or not, you will need to emphasize how the action supports the audience's beliefs or benefits them in your message.

(4) What will persuade them?

In order to achieve your goal of communication as much as possible, the content of your communication will have to be very persuasive, and that requires you to emphasize your audience's benefits during communication, which is what we call the "WIIFT" principle to draw on

的兴趣？如果兴趣很高，那么你可以很快切入正题；相反则需要考虑采取咨询或参与性强的沟通方式唤起其兴趣。

听众可能带有哪些偏见，这些偏见是正面的还是负面的？对于正面或中性听众态度，沟通者可以沟通中进一步强化听众立场；对于负面的听众态度，则要采取一些技巧来开展交流，例如将你的要求降低到最小，以一个试点计划来替代全盘计划等。

从听众的角度来看，你期望的行动对他们来说难易如何？对听众认为困难的任务，可以尝试把行动目标分解，并尽可能地降低难度。然而不论难易，都应在沟通的中强调听众利益。

（4）什么能够说服他们？

增强沟通说服力，要求在沟通中强调听众利益，即"WIIFT"策略，同时善用你自己的可信度去提高自己的说服力，并且善用遣词造句、构建信息的技巧。

your own credibility and to structure the way you organize your message.

The "WIIFT" principle is short for "what's in it for them", which means you need to persuade with audience benefits and that include tangible benefits, career or task benefits, ego benefits, personality benefits and group benefits. You may also need to figure out the best angle to put forward the benefits that most suit your audience.

"WIIFT"原则要求展现听众利益，包括但不限于具体有形的利益、职业收获、自我价值利益、个性利益以及群体利益等。

Also, as we have discussed in chapter 2.3, your credibility is an important element in the act of communication, so you need to apply it as a persuasive tool. As we already know that there are five factors affecting your credibility, you should also remember that the less your audience is involved in the topic or issue, the more important your credibility is as a factor for persuasion. Some common techniques to apply your credibility include creating shared values and common ground, expressing reciprocating goodwill, exhibiting your rank and expertise, etc.

提高可信度以增强说服力。前文分析了影响可信度的因素，并且听众参与度越低，沟通者的可信度就越重要。沟通者可以通过与沟通对象建立共同立场和共同价值观、表达良好的互利互惠意愿、展示自己身份地位和专业知识水平等增强可信度。

And finally, there are also some message structuring techniques to strengthen your persuasion. For example, you can always emphasize audience benefits in your opening and closing, and you can use a two-sided approach instead of a one-sided one for a prior or controversial subject, because the audience will hear your positive arguments more clearly after their concern have been addressed, and you will appear more reasonable and fair-minded.

利用一些遣词造句、构建信息的技巧来增加自己的说服力，例如总是在交流的开场白和结束语当中强调听众可能取得的收益，对于比较重大或有争议性的问题采取双向并举结构而非单向阐述来说服。

3. Message Strategy

Message strategy is about how you structure your message. Novice communicators usually create "data dump", which means that they simply express the ideas in the order they happen to occur to them because it is easy for them, but it can be hard for the audience to absorb. Instead, you should stand back and think about what you want them to take away by emphasizing and organizing your ideas.

In order to do this, you may ask yourself two questions: How can you emphasize your message? And how to organize your message?

(1) Emphasize your beginnings and endings.

As we already know seizing audience's attention is one of the most important things at the beginning and the end of your message, so if you state your main point upfront, it is called the "direct approach"; and if you save it for the end, it is called the "indirect approach". We can choose either direct approach or indirect approach to adapt different situations (See Figure 8.3).

3. 信息策略

信息策略是指如何组织信息。"堆积信息"很容易，但听众却不容易接收。沟通者应事先思考希望听众接收到哪些信息，再据此来强调和构建沟通表达。

信息策略的核心在于：如何强调信息？如何组织信息？

（1）重视开头和结尾。

吸引听众注意力在沟通的开头和结尾部分至关重要。在沟通开始部分提出主要观点被称为"直接叙述法"；在结尾部分提出主要观点被称为"间接叙述法。"

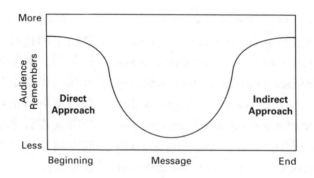

Figure 8.3　Audience's Memory Curve
图 8.3　听众记忆曲线

In general, use the direct approach whenever possible, because in most business cases, the audience would prefer such an approach as it improves their comprehension and saves time. By contrast, the indirect approach leaves your main point to the end, making your message look like a mystery story. Many of us use the indirect approach by habit or academic training, but in real-time business communication, perhaps you should use this approach with caution because it is harder to follow for the audience and it takes longer time to understand.

For example, when your company decides to increase the advertisement invest for a new product, you can use direct approach.

通常在商务交流当中应尽量使用直接叙述法,因为这对听众来说易于理解并能节省时间;与之相反,间接叙述法则是在沟通最后才提出主要观点,这不仅提高了听众理解的难度也更费时,因此应谨慎使用。

下面将举例说明直接叙述法的场景运用。

Example:

We decide to increase the advertisement invest for our new product (important message) for the following reasons: First, our competitors have increased their invest in the product. Second, the new functions of the product are not recognized by our target market so far. Third, we have enough budget to put money in it.

In this case, by using direct approach, audience get your point in the beginning, which will benefit their comprehension of your idea. Also, it saves time and make the communication more effective.

But direct approach doesn't apply to all the occasions. For things which have negative effect of audience or the communicator who is not so credible, they can choose the indirect approach.

在上例中,直接叙述法把重要的事情放在开头部分,从而让听众在开场就明白你的观点,可以节约更多的时间,提高沟通效率。

并非所有的情况都适合开门见山亮出观点,特别是对听众沟通负面信息的时候可以采用间接叙述法。

> **Example:**
> The winter of Internet is coming. And our company goes down in this quarter. To save cost and be more competitive, we decide to cut the research engineering team (important message).

According to the audience's memory curve (Figure 8.3), if you adopt a direct approach, the beginning part of your message is better remembered; while if you adopt an indirect approach, the ending part of your message is better remembered. Therefore, you should pay attention to the following tips.

① Never "bury" important messages in the middle of your communication.

② State your main conclusion emphatically at the beginning or the end, according to your choice of approach.

③ Use communicating techniques to keep your audience's attention in the middle of your communication.

(2) How to organize message?

In addition to emphasize your conclusion, you also need to organize your main ideas in the body of your communication.

If your main purpose of communication is to inform, i.e. "to tell information" as in contrast of "to persuade", then you need to decide how to chunk the information so that you can highlight your prior points. Possible organizational patterns include "point by point", "question by question", "step by step", "alternative by alternative", etc.

If your purpose of communication is to

听众记忆曲线显示，沟通的开头或结尾时最容易被听众记住的部分。

绝对不要将重要信息放在沟通的中间部分。

将主要结论放在开始或结尾来进行明确的传达。

在沟通的中间阶段，运用一定的技巧维持听众兴趣。

（2）如何组织信息。

除了在结尾处强调结论之外，还需要在中间部分进行信息的组织。

如果你的沟通目标是"告知"而非"说服"，你就需要把内容进行归纳，突出要点。

如果你的沟通目标是

persuade, which is common for "selling" situations, then you need to find an organization pattern that works best for your situation. In these cases, your option may include "list of recommendations (direct approach)", "list of benefits (direct approach)", "problems and possible solutions (indirect approach)", etc.

4. Channel Choice Strategy

Communication channels are the means through which people in an organization communicate. Choosing channels or media is of great importance in completing various tasks, because using an inappropriate channel for a task or interaction can lead to negative consequences. Complex messages require combination use of communication channels that facilitate interaction to ensure clarity.

In Chapter 6, we discussed various communication channels, including:

(1) Face-to-face channels such as meetings, public appearances, live web chats, events and open houses offer the advantage of immediate feedback. In managerial context, these channels generally contribute to the effort of becoming the credible and trustworthy public face of your company — the first step toward developing a long-term relationship with your customers.

(2) Interactive social media channels such as blogs, discussion forums, WeChat (Twitter) and Online Video Sharing Websit (YouTube) also offer

"说服",你需要组织对你观点有支持的内容,说明推荐(直接法)、利益价值(直接法)、问题与对策(间接法)等。

4. 渠道选择策略

沟通渠道指组织沟通所选择的路径和方式。选择何种沟通渠道至关重要,错误的渠道选择将会带来负面后果。复杂信息需要将各种沟通渠道组合运用。

第6章我们讨论了多种沟通渠道,包括:

(1)面对面渠道。

(2)互动社交媒体渠道。

immediacy and the benefit of two-way communication. They also offer the added advantage of shareability.

(3) Traditional print advertising channels such as brochures, flyers, newspapers and direct mail offer a key advantage reader credibility.

(4) Traditional broadcast channels such as radio and TV advertising offer wide range and the ability to reach new audience members.

In business, making modifications is a normal part of the recursive process in media selection, especially when the chosen channel doesn't produce results. From marketing perspective, experimenting with a new channel is also wise. Assess it carefully before you commit to using it regularly. Remember that your customers are always "watching," and erratic moves run the risk of reflecting poorly on your company. Also, marketing managers need to resist the temptation to engage in "knee-jerk marketing," or the tendency to forge ahead with a new channel just because "everybody" seems to be talking about it. The truth is, you cannot spread your message everywhere; you have to make strategic choices based on your communication goals and budget.

5. Culture Strategy

Culture is another important aspect that can influence your communication strategy. The term "different cultures" could refer to

（3）传统硬广告渠道。

（4）传统广播电视渠道。

企业的媒体选择始终处于动态调整的过程，当原有的媒体渠道效果不好，尝试一个新渠道未尝不是明智的选择。然而这种尝试需要建立在谨慎评估基础上，以免给消费者带来负面影响。营销经理既要避免本能式的渠道选择也要避免随大流，应该基于沟通目标和预算作出战略选择。

5. 文化策略

"文化"同样是影响沟通策略的重要因素。"文化差异"不仅指不同国家之间的

not only different countries, but also different regions, industries, organizations, genders, ethnic groups or work groups, i.e. anywhere that has a common code of behaviors and beliefs. Therefore, while communicating, you should take these common codes and beliefs of your audience into consideration and make communication strategies accordingly. The most commonly-seen elements in such codes include:

(1) Communication style.

Different communication styles tend to work better in different cultures. For example, group-oriented cultures may favor join styles, while individualistic cultures may favor sell styles; autocratic cultures may favor tell styles, while democratic cultures may favor consult styles.

(2) Credibility.

The five factors affecting your credibility — rank, goodwill, expertise, image and common ground — have different value and priorities in different cultures. While dealing with audience of different cultural backgrounds, you may need to put emphasize on different aspects while communicating.

(3) Audience analysis.

Different cultures have different attitudes toward age, gender, educational level, etc. Based on cultural expectations about rank, authority or group definition, you may need to make audience analysis including primary audiences (key influencers), secondary audiences and hidden audiences.

(4) Gender-based tendencies.

Sometimes it is necessary to take the

文化差异，还可以是不同宗教、行业、机构、性别、民族以及工作团体之间的文化差异。

以下是一些常见的文化差异因素：

（1）沟通风格。

不同的文化可能会趋向于采用不同的沟通风格。集体倾向性文化偏好参与式，个体倾向性文化偏好说服式；专制倾向性文化偏好命令式；民主倾向性文化偏好咨询式。

（2）可信度。

影响沟通可信度的五个因素在不同的文化中有着不同的重要性和优先度。

（3）听众分析。

不同的文化对于年龄、性别、教育水平等因素的态度可能不尽相同。应结合文化背景对社会层级、权威和团体定义的期望进行听众分析。

（4）基于性别的偏好。

听众的性别也具有重要

cultural difference between men and women into consideration. For example, research shows that men tend to take arguments straight-forwardly, while women more personally; men seek quick authoritative decisions, while women prefer consensus building; men use stronger languages even when they're not sure, while women use more qualified language even when they're sure, etc.

影响。男性和女性群体之间的文化差异会对其沟通风格产生影响。

【Conclusion】本章小结

In this chapter, we studied the different strategies and approaches to managerial communication, and discussed the strategies from different perspectives. After learning this chapter, the students should be able to identify key influence factors for various communication scenarios and improve communication skills accordingly.

【Case Study】案例讨论

The Mercedes-Benz customer who turned her complaint about a dealer's handling of an oil leak in her brand new CLS 300 into a viral social media video got more than 200 million hits on Internet. It became one of the hottest issues on crisis communication in April 2019.

The woman, surnamed Wang, picked up her 660,000 yuan (US $98,690) car at Shaanxi-based Xi'an Lizhixing Auto at the end of March, 2019. Before she had driven one kilometer from the showroom to her home, she said in the video filmed weeks later as she sat frustrated and crying on a showroom Mercedes, an oil leak warning appeared.

Miss Wang claimed Lizhixing Auto had changed its position on her complaint several times, from promising a new car, to offering her a refund, and finally to an offer of a new engine. She refused angrily, because a car that has repaired with its engine is a bad signal to quality. She thought it is unreasonable for her to bear the loss. 10 days past, no progress occurred. When she made her further complaint, she asked to speak to senior management, but sales staff did not supply the information. After attempts to involve the authorities failed, Wang said she had no other option than to use social media to be heard.

On April 9, she sat on the hood of a car and cried to staff and other customers about how she was treated. After her video blew up a storm on the Internet, market regulators in Xi'an, the capital of Shaanxi province, launched an investigation, the *People's Daily* reported.

On April 13, she met the general manager of the showroom, in the presence of market supervisors. The negotiations failed because Wang said she felt the dealer was arrogant and lacked sincerity. "I think everybody, whether it is a big company or an individual, has rights to have dialogue on an equal basis," Wang told Thepaper.cn.

Later, Miss Wang issued an open letter to Lizhixing, the showroom, questioning the financial service fee charged by the showroom. She said the dealer persuaded her to take out a loan to buy the car, which involved a financial service fee of 15 thousand rmb. The money is required to transfer to a personal account without any receipt. This aroused another hot hit on Internet. Mercedes-Benz China quickly replied to the open letter, claiming that Mercedes-Benz China had never charging financial service fee, which is also illegal to the showroom to doing so.

The tax authorities said they were checking Lizhixing Auto's affairs, while the China Banking and Insurance Regulatory Commission asked its branch in Beijing to investigate whether Mercedes-Benz China's financial business had charged other customers service fees through its dealers, state news agency Xinhua said.

Several days later, on Tuesday, Xi'an Lizhixing Auto agreed to provide a replacement car and refund 15,000 yuan it charged her for financial service fees on the loan she took out to buy her CLS 300, Thepaper.cn reported.

Mercedes-Benz representatives witnessed the signing of the agreement and invited Wang to visit the company's production base in Germany.

It also said it had suspended the showroom's license.

"We are launching a compliance investigation of the dealer," Mercedes said. "Before the conclusion is made, we decided to suspend the showroom."

"If any practice of this dealer is found to have violated regulations or compliance rules, we will terminate its showroom license."

"In the past, they did not treat me equally. Perhaps they thought they are a big company and I am just nobody," she said. "Now, I am receiving so much attention from Internet users. This result is probably not what I expected, but am satisfied with it."

(Adapted from Internet news)[1]

Questions:
(1) What is the context at the beginning of this complain?
(2) What is the negative impact on Mercedes company?
(3) Construct a communication factor decomposition diagram to analyze the case. Use panoramic analysis to propose communication strategies for Mercedes company.

【Study Questions】课后问题

1. What are the communication strategies to make managerial communication successful?
2. How to set communication objectives?
3. What are the four approaches of communication style? How to determine your approach to your audience?

---

1 Adapted from: https://ph.news.yahoo.com/chinese-woman-whose-mercedes-benz-121727053.html
http://bbs.chinadaily.com.cn/forum.php?mod=viewthread&tid=1902877.

Section 2

Practices on Management Communication

第 2 篇 管理沟通实践

Chapter 9　Team Communication

第9章　团队沟通

Whether you are in business, retail, healthcare, education or other industries, when teamwork goes well, it distributes the work among team members in ways that make it easier to reach goals and excel in the industry. Good communication skills are integral to any team's success and the overall success of the business.

In this chapter, you will:
- understand the features of effective team communication;
- learn the types of team conflicts;
- comprehend skills on team communication.

无论在哪个商业领域，当团队合作顺畅时，组织更容易实现目标，并在行业中表现优秀。良好的沟通技能是任何团队和商业成功的关键。

通过学习本章，你可以：了解团队沟通的特征；理解团队冲突的类型；掌握团队沟通技能。

9.1　What Is Team Communication

一、什么是团队沟通

Almost everyone has team-working experiences. Within those teams, communication is crucial between all members, regardless of what role each person plays. Whether it is between two teammates on a sports team or two managers in a corporate office, communication is vital to success.

在任何一种团队中，无论扮演什么角色，成员间的沟通非常重要。

1. Effective Communication

1. 有效沟通

Teammates must develop trust, since it is not automatic. Accordingly, members must

团队成员需要培养信任，应该能够公开地交流。团队的

communicate more openly than they normally would in everyday life. There must be honesty on all ends of the team, since withholding the truth could damage the team's integrity. Team members should always share information and feelings between each other. This allows for total trust between the team members.

2. Importance of Communication

Research has found that team work on a project is much more effective than a single person spending all of his/her time doing the same thing. However, without communication, the three-plus team members can be as useless as if the project went untouched.

Teams that fail to communicate effectively wind up wasting time and energy doing busy work and work that is not required. These team members also have barriers in understanding each other and the aim of the work. This often leads to conflicts within the team and lack of trust between group members. Team members in groups that fail to communicate effectively wind up not understanding what makes themselves more efficient, because they fail to get feedback from everyone else in the group, and there is no one else that they can compare their work to.

3. Benefits of Team Communication

Teams that communicate complete projects in a quicker and more efficient amount of time than others. They also are more accurate in their work than others. Effective communication also allows

每一位成员都必须诚实，因为隐瞒真相会损害团队的整体利益。团队成员应该经常互相分享信息和感受，这就要求团队成员之间完全信任。

2. 沟通的重要性

研究发现，多人共事比一个人单打独斗更有效率。但如果缺乏沟通，团队成员可能会无所适从。

没有有效沟通的团队会把时间和精力浪费在不重要的工作上，因为他们缺乏对需要做什么的理解。团队成员的误解往往导致集团内部的冲突和集团成员之间缺乏信任。

3. 团队沟通的益处

沟通让团队更有时间效率，有效的沟通还可以让团队成员了解他们的角色以及团队中其他人的角色。

team members to understand their roles and the roles of everyone else on the team. It also gives room for understanding among the team members for what needs to be done.

Research shows that good communication, mixed with strong organizational support, competence among the group leaders and clear group objectives can lead to the highest level of success in teams. Among those factors, good communication has shown to be of top importance for success.

良好的沟通、强有力的组织支持、团队领导者能力、明确的团队目标，可以帮助团队实现成功。在这些因素中，良好的沟通是最为重要的。

4. Roles in Teams

Individual members can play multiple roles within teams, and these roles can change during the team's work. Positive roles and actions can help the teams build loyalty, resolve conflicts, and achieves its goals, while negative roles and actions could hurt the team's product and progress.

4. 团队角色

个体可以在团队中扮演多个角色，并且这些角色可以在团队的工作中不断变化。积极的角色和行动可以帮助团队实现目标，而消极的角色和行动可能会损害团队的产出和进度。

Positive behaviors:

Encouraging participation — demonstrating openness and acceptance, recognizing the contributions.

Relieving tensions — joking and suggesting to relieve conflicting emotions.

Checking feelings — caring about others' feelings, willing to share thoughts.

Solving interpersonal problems — opening discussions.

Listening actively — show understanding when listening.

Negative behaviors:

Blocking — disagreeing with everything that is proposed.

> Dominating — trying to run the team by ordering or insisting on one's own way.
>
> Clowning — making unproductive jokes and diverting the team from the task.
>
> Over speaking — taking every opportunity to be the first to speak.
>
> Withdrawing — being silent in group meetings, not contributing.

9.2 Team Conflict and Effective Communication

二、团队冲突与有效沟通

Conflicts are going to arise in any group of intelligent people who care about their task. Yet many of us feel so uncomfortable with conflict that we pretend it doesn't exist. However, unacknowledged conflicts rarely go away.

冲突无处不在。然而，许多人对冲突感到非常不安，以至于视而不见。

Although constructive conflicts are regarded as favorable factors for innovation spirit, extreme and destructive conflicts between your employees can negatively affect the productivity of your entire department. Although you expect your employees to be grown adults and manage their issues on their own, there are times when it is advantageous for a leader to step in and handle the situation. Although you may feel that it is not your place, you should understand that it is a leader's job to handle conflicts in an appropriate way to maintain positive corporate culture and promote positive teamwork.

建设性的冲突有助于鼓励创新精神，然而激烈的破坏性冲突会影响整个部门的工作效率。管理者有时需要以一种适当方式介入，保持良好的公司文化、推动积极的团队合作。

1. Different Types of Team Conflicts

1. 不同的团队冲突类型

(1) Conflict over positions, strategies or opinions.

When team members holding different

（1）立场、策略或意见之冲突。如果团队中有强烈的两

opinions, or even hostile opinions can't reach consensus in a meeting, a leader needs to make sure everyone understand the other people's stand and information, looking for concerns or goals that people have in common. In most cases this becomes the new focus and it turns the situation from conflict to problem solving.

(2) Mistrust or uneven communication.

In a team, if some people actively dominate the conversation while others remain silent or distracted, a leader should try to create even opportunity of speaking. A simple practice is to appoint an observer whose job is to focus on the process of discussion. If the discussion gets out of tracks — it might be rising angers or diverting from real task — the process observer is allowed to remind or correct.

(3) Personality clashes.

Different personalities will cause conflicts among team members. DISC, MBTI, or another behavioral assessment tool are useful to help people better understand each other and learn to work together. They can also provide a common frame of reference for dealing with individual differences.

2. Steps in Conflict Resolution

Conflict can be constructive for a team when it is solved properly. The challenges for leaders are how to intervene through effective communication. Dealing successfully with conflict requires attention both to the issues and to people's feelings. The following are some tips on

种以上不同意见无法统一，领导者应该让团队成员应耐心倾听以明确各方立场和方案，努力寻找共识，变冲突为问题解决。

（2）不信任或沟通不畅。

在一个团队中，如果一些人主动主导谈话，而另一些人保持沉默或分心，领导者应该尝试创造甚至是发言的机会。可以在团队中设置观察员，就观察到的影响团队讨论的现象提醒注意。

（3）个性冲突。

管理者可以借助一些量表分析团队成员的个性，让他们更了解彼此需要，并尝试减少个体分歧，学习共同工作。

2. 冲突处理的步骤

合理处理冲突对团队健康发展有利。领导者的挑战是如何在干预中有效沟通。成功地处理冲突需要同时关注问题和人们的感受。

conflict resolution procedures.

The following steps are recommended in conflict resolution.

Steps in Conflict Resolution

Make sure the people involved really disagree. Sometimes different conversational styles, differing interpretations of data or faulty inferences, create apparent conflicts when no real disagreement exists. Sometimes someone who's under a lot of pressure may explode, but may not in fact be angry at the person who receives the explosion.

Check to see that everyone's information is correct. People may act on personal biases or opinions rather than data.

Discover the needs each person is trying to meet. Determining the real needs makes it possible to see a new solution.

Search for alternatives. In a team, too few alternatives often lock people into conflicts. To solve an important problem, the team needs to follow a formal process to generate alternatives before moving on to a decision. Brainstorming is widely used in organizations.

Repair negative feelings. If people's feelings have been hurt in conflicts, the team needs to deal with those feelings to resolve the conflicts constructively. Trust is built on receptiveness. When people feel respected can they work on the solution of conflicts together.

9.3 Skills on Effective Team Communication

1. Set Clear and Reachable Goals and Work Allocation

Good communication is crucial in setting goals and work allocation. The team leader communicates the goals of the task to all team members, and make work allocation properly. This means nobody has to be responsible for or

三、有效团队沟通的技巧

1. 设定清晰目标与合理分工

沟通是达成沟通目标的重要因素。团队负责人将项目要达成的效果和要求告知成员，并根据成员的能力特长进行分工，并完美组合。

be able to do everything. While one person excels at customer care, another person has outstanding presentation skills. Clear communication makes these things evident so that deadlines are less stressful and objectives are met and exceeded with ease.

2. Greater Efficiency, Better Solutions

When each team player knows his or her role in serving clients or meeting a deadline, all are free to focus on only their own tasks, without worrying about what everyone else is doing. Clear communication also means communicating with teammates when you are not able to complete your tasks, so the team can come up with solutions before the situation escalates and the team process breaks down. Communication helps you maintain efficiency under a variety of circumstances and conditions.

3. Positive Work Relationships

Effective communication foster trust between teammates, and creates an environment for positive professional relationships. When teammates know each other well, they become acquainted with each others' strengths, weaknesses, tendencies and thinking patterns, which makes it easier to work together on a task.

4. Creating a Culture of Celebration

Good team communication skills are not simply about assigning tasks or troubleshooting

良好的沟通能力将使成员之间的合作更为顺畅。

2. 促进提升效率和提出更好的方案

当每一位团队成员都知道如何更好地为客户服务或按时达成工作目标要求，工作和沟通就会更为顺畅。清楚的沟通还包括及时与团队成员沟通不能达成目标的情况，以获得其他成员的帮助避免整个任务失败。

3. 积极的工作关系

沟通有助于建立相互信任的工作关系和环境。当团队成员对彼此的优势、弱点、喜好、思维模式等更了解的时候，更容易建立起默契、稳定的合作关系。

4. 创造相互肯定的文化

好的团队沟通技能并非局限于分配工作和解决问题，

problems. Communication is also about creating a culture of celebration in the workplace. Teammates and team leaders who notice achievements of their peers and employees take the time to communicate and celebrate together. Improvement is noticed, congratulated and encouraged, as well, which creates an environment where employees want to be their best on the job and maintain a growth mindset.

同样包括创造一个工作场所的"认同文化"，团队领导和成员能够发现团队中的成就和个人进步，并一起庆祝、鼓舞，最终激发每位成员进步的愿望。

5. Reducing and Diffusing Conflicts

Whenever a group of people work together, conflict is likely to arise at one time or another. Whether conflict is due to unfair expectations, irresponsibility or personal misunderstanding, good team communication skills let everyone have a voice and feel heard. When it is safe to express thoughts clearly, honestly and tactfully, it is easier to move forward with a solution that has everyone's best interest at heart. Once on the other side of conflict, a team with good communication skills may even feel stronger for overcoming the hurdle.

5. 减少和分化冲突

冲突在工作中无法完全避免，良好的团队沟通可以让每个人的声音和想法得到清晰、坦诚、策略的表达时，更容易达成一个符合各方利益的解决方案。合理的冲突让团队更强大。

【Conclusion】本章小结

In this chapter, features and types of team communication are discussed.

To resolve team conflicts, first make sure that the people involved really disagree. Next, check to see that everyone's information is correct. Discover the needs that each person is trying to meet. The presenting problem that surfaces as the subject of dissension may or may not be the real problem. Search for alternatives. Last but not least, repair negative feelings.

Effective communication will help team members to set clear and reachable goals, make reasonable work allocation, improve productivity, create positive work relationships and team culture, and reduce conflicts.

【Case Study】案例讨论

Coopi is a large commercial supermarket in US. At the time, there was a major conflict occurring between employees and they had formed two opposing groups. Each side did not get along with the other and they had banded together in an "us vs. them" mentality. Furthermore, the employees involved were resistant to solving any issues and the supervisor, along with other management staff, was well aware of the problem, but chose not to intervene.

When Tom Ingren was promoted to department supervisor, one of his goals was to make the department more cohesive. There were a variety of approaches that he could have taken, but he wanted to know more about his own conflict style, so Tom received approval to attend a conflict management seminar, where he learned that, due to the fact that he looks for ways to solve problems in which an optimum result is provided for everyone, his style is that of a "collaborator". This means that he needs to pay close attention to realizing that conflict can be resolved without damaging relationships and, as a manager, it is his responsibility to identify and help resolve employee conflicts.

One of the most important areas that needed improvement within the team was communication. He immediately implemented weekly staff meetings, along with weekly individual meetings. This way, not only did the entire staff hear the same information in a consistent manner, but would give them a sense of togetherness as they had an honest discussion about the pain points in their department. The individual meetings were equally significant, since it not only gave employees an opportunity to privately talk with me about their concerns and goals, but it allowed Tom time to review what needed improvement, as well as provide positive feedback and realistic suggestions for how they could help decrease the problems.

Some of the conflicts were a result of certain tasks that had always been performed by only a handful of staff. There was a perception of power because of this and it had not changed in many years. Tom took this as an opportunity to cross-train all of the employees in the different job responsibilities. This helped with leveling out the playing field and was also useful for when workers were out due to illness or vacation. When Tom met with the department, their overall reaction was positive, even from those who had exclusively done these tasks.

Finally, in an effort to clarify rules and procedures, Tom and his colleagues created a departmental handbook that everyone had a hand in providing feedback on and creating. This helped tremendously since most procedures were never written down and each person had their own way of performing tasks. In many instances, staff had no clue that some co-workers were duplicating and even triplicating certain steps. Each member of the team then signed an agreement to follow these processes while also respecting other employees. Overall, this streamlined the workflow and made many tasks easier, which made them a happier team.

Conflict is going to happen in any organization, but how employees decide to deal with it, along with how management gets involved, is vital to maintaining a productive and positive work environment.

Questions:
(1) What techniques did Tom use when dealing with conflicts in work place?
(2) What are your comments and suggestions?

【Study Questions】课后问题

1. What is the feature of team communication?
2. What are different types of team conflict? How effective communication can reduce team conflicts?
3. What are skills on effective team communication?

Chapter 10　Crisis Communication

第10章　危机沟通

The purpose of crisis communication is to protect and defend an individual, company, or organization out of crisis status, in order to reduce loss, and reestablish its reputation.

In this chapter, you will:

- know the definitions of crisis and types of crisis;
- understand the requirements of crisis communication;
- comprehend tactics of crisis communication in the pre-crisis, in-crisis and post-crisis status.

危机沟通旨在保护危机中的个人、公司或组织，以减少损失并挽回声誉。

学完本章后，你将了解危机的定义与分类；理解危机沟通的需求分析；掌握危机前、危机中、危机后的危机沟通技巧。

10.1　Definition and Classification of Crisis

一、危机的定义与分类

Crisis can be defined as a series of specific, unexpected events that creates high levels of uncertainty and threat or perceived threat to an organization.

危机是能够对于组织产生不确定性和威胁的一系列事件。

Definitions on Crisis

Hermann (1972) presented the classic definition of crisis: "A crisis is a situation that threatens high priority goals of the decision making unit, restricts the amount of time available for response before the decision is transformed and surprises members of the decision making unit by its

---

occurrence."

Fearn Banks(1996) considered crisis as "a major occurrence with a potentially negative outcome affecting an organization, company, or industry, as well as publics, products, services or good name. It interrupts normal business transactions and can sometimes threaten the existence of the organization."

Seeger, Sellnow, & Ulmer (1998) thought crisis is "a specific, unexpected and non-routine organizationally based event or series of events which creates high levels of uncertainty and threat or perceived threat to an organization's high priority goals."

Coombs (1999) observes that "crisis is an event that is an unpredictable, major threat that can have a negative effect on the organization, industry, or stakeholders if handled improperly."

Crisis can be divided into several types within different dimensions. According to the Situational Crisis Communication Theory posited by W. Timothy Coombs, three "crisis clusters", or types of crises, have been identified including the victim cluster, the accidental cluster and the intentional cluster (See Table 10.1).

根据场景危机沟通理论，危机可分为被动接受类、意外发生类和主动造成类。

In the victim cluster, the organization is viewed as a victim and not attributed as the cause of the crisis. In the accidental cluster, the organization has been nominally attributed as the cause of the crisis, but the situation is generally viewed by stakeholders as being unintentional or simply accidental. In the intentional cluster, all or most of the attributions for the crisis is given to the organization.

在被动接受类的危机中，组织被看作危机的受害者；在意外发生类的危机中，组织被看作危机的制造者，但造成危机的动机并非故意而是过失；在主动造成类的危机中，组织对于危机的产生负有主要责任。

Table 10.1   SCCT Crisis Types by Crisis Cluster
表 10.1   场景危机沟通理论的危机分类

Types	Definitions	Features	Examples
Victim cluster	The organization is a victim of the crisis	Weak attributions of crisis responsibility and mild reputational threat	Natural disaster, rumor, workplace violence
Accidental cluster	The organizational actions leading the crisis were unintentional	Minimal attribution of crisis responsibility and moderate reputational threat	Technical-error accidents, misoperation
Intentional cluster	The organization knowingly placed people at risk, took inappropriate actions or violated a law/regulation	Strong attributions of crisis responsibility and severe reputational threat	Human error products, organizational misdeed

In business, the crises that enterprises may come across in different stage of life cycle include marketing crisis, human resource crisis, credit crisis, financial crisis, brand crisis, safety crisis, etc.

Crisis can also have other classifications depending on its attributes. According to its predictability, the crisis can be divided into predictable and unpredictable, such as plane crash is an unpredictable event for the airline. According to the degree of human participation, the crisis can be divided into artificial crisis and non-human crisis. For example, the factory fire caused by technical workers' operational errors should be considered as artificial crisis. According to the speed of the crisis, the crisis can be divided into

企业不同成长阶段遇到的危机包括营销危机、人力资源危机、信用危机、财产危机、品牌危机、安全危机等。

根据其可预见性，危机可分为可预测的与不可预测的危机。

根据人为参与程度，危机可分为人为危机和非人为危机。

根据危机发生速度，危机可分为突发性危机和潜伏性危机。

sudden crisis and latent crisis. There are fewer signs before sudden crisis, while latent crises may have minor problems at the beginning.

A crisis in business is any occurrence that interferes with business operations and that draws public scrutiny and media attention, and may be anything from serving a customer tainted food to finding a major error in accounting. In business, news of crisis spreads fast and a business that is not prepared to handle crisis could be in danger of tarnishing its reputation. Therefore, knowing how to handle a crisis when it arises could be necessary to a business's survival.

10.2　Crisis Communication Targets

Communication is an important part of any business's crisis management. When a crisis occurs, an organization needs to communicate with internal group and external group. Internal group includes staff, senior executives and functional departments, while external group involves customers, investors, distributors, government, media and other stakeholders. In crisis communication, main communication targets are simplified into internal staff, customer, media and other stakeholders.

1. Internal Crisis Communication

When crisis breaks out, stabilizing internal staffs is acknowledged as a key action. The communication process needs to be in-time and

任何干扰企业运营、引起公众监督和媒体关注的事件都可能成为企业危机，例如食品安全、会计失真等。在商业领域，危机信息传播很快，缺乏危机应对的企业将可能面临名誉受损的风险。因此，了解危机处理对企业至关重要。

二、危机沟通对象

沟通在企业危机管理中具有重要作用。危机发生后，组织需要与内部和外部进行沟通。

1. 危机的内部沟通

与员工的危机沟通需要强调情况通知主动性、统一的对外沟通渠道以及全体参

effective. The internal crisis communication requires proactive notification, which means the organization should release crisis-related information through various internal channels before the staffs receive it from other channels.

Keep a unified channel for external communication ensures an official department or spokesman that convey relevant messages to media or external communication targets. Only in this way can they form and maintain the authority and establish effective channels for external communication. The idea of full participation is to motivate all functional units and all staff to solve the crisis and become a participant of organization or enterprise management team. With diversified suggestions and feedback from staff, the crisis management team will gain a more accurate general picture of crisis situation.

When communicating with internal staff, it is necessary to adopt various formal channels and informal channels to convey information so that they can identify the current situation of organization or enterprise. Communication feedback channel should also be provided for immediate message exchange and decision making. When crisis occurs, senior executives should be involved as soon as possible. The organization or enterprise must deliver differentiated information to staffs from different levels according to the actual situation and pay close attention to the vital interests of staffs to remove their worries.

与的意识。组织应在员工通过其他途径了解危机情况前告知员工危机相关信息。

组织应采取统一的对外沟通渠道，确定官方对外沟通部门或者新闻发言人发布信息，从而形成官方发布的权威性，有利于建立有效的对外沟通渠道。全体参与的意识需要推动各职能部门和全体员工参与到危机解决中。通过多样的建议与反馈，协助危机管理团队形成对于当前危机的情况的更为准确的整体观念。

要尽可能采取多种正式渠道、非正式渠道向员工传达信息，使其了解危机的情况。还应提供沟通反馈渠道，以便立即进行信息交流和决策。当危机发生时，高级管理人员应尽快介入。组织或企业必须根据实际情况向不同层次的员工传递差异化的信息，密切关注员工的切身利益，消除员工的顾虑。

2. External Crisis Communication

External communication targets include customer, media, and other stakeholders.

(1) Customer.

In business crisis, customers have the highest possibility to become one of the main victims. One purpose of crisis communication is to comfort and compensate customers to stabilize the market.

When crisis occur, the organization should make direct contact with relevant customer. Convey messages about crisis including the problems and the possible consequences, also the possible development of crisis and attitude towards the whole event.

(2) Media.

In the information era, the response of media towards crisis has become more efficient and more rapid. Information channel become more diverse and connected in a global scope. Under normal circumstances, media is not a victim of crisis, however the content and attitude of media about the crisis will affect the public's perception of the crisis. The media can play a positive effect on the crisis, and may also play a negative one. Therefore, organization or enterprises must handle the relationship with media during the crisis.

(3) Other stakeholders.

Stakeholders include investors, shareholders, lenders, government administrations, etc. Stakeholders are mostly representatives who are

2. 危机的外部沟通

危机的外部沟通对象包括消费者、媒体以及其他利益相关者。

（1）消费者。

在企业危机中，消费者最有可能成为主要的受害者。与消费者的危机沟通主要目的在于安慰并补偿，从而稳定市场。

危机爆发后，组织或企业应当与有关客户直接接触以了解有关情况，如发生的问题及其危害，事态发展可能性，对于事件的态度等。

（2）媒体。

在信息时代，媒体对于危机的反应迅速且高效，信息传播的渠道更为多样化且全球化。媒体对危机报道的内容和态度将极大程度地影响公众对危机的意见，因而对危机管理可能存在正面效应或负面效应。因此组织或企业在危机应对中必须妥善处理与媒体的关系。

（3）其他利益相关者。

利益相关者包括投资人、股东、贷款人等，多为与企业命运紧密相关的代表，企

highly relevant with the fate of the organization or enterprise. The impact of the crisis will have a direct or indirect influence on the stakeholders.

10.3 Crisis Communication Strategies

Communication is an important part of any business's crisis management. In this section, crisis communication strategies are discussed according to the process of pre-crisis, in-crisis and post-crisis stages.

1. Pre-Crisis

As Murphy's Law stated: "Anything that can go wrong will go wrong." It is necessary for an organization to get prepared for crisis. In the pre-crisis stage, identifying possible crises and developing a crisis communication plan are very important.

(1) Identifying the crises.

In business, crises could be very complicated, combining internal crises and external crises. It could be property damage, accidents or incidents that injure employees and other people, issues with the quality of products or services, criminal investigations or other legal actions such as lawsuits against the company, or even natural disasters.

Making analysis and identifying crises as accurate as possible are the fundamental steps in pre-crisis communication management. Brainstorming is commonly used in crises identification.

业发生危机后的冲击将有极大可能直接或间接影响到其利益。

三、危机沟通策略

危机沟通贯穿于组织危机管理的全过程，包括危机前、危机中、危机后三阶段。

1. 危机前

在沟通方面，危机发生前的预防工作主要是识别危机和制定危机沟通计划。

（1）识别危机。

商业环境中的危机可能非常复杂，包含各种可能的情况。

在危机前的沟通管理中，应尽可能准确地进行分析和识别危机。头脑风暴是最为常用的方法。

Brainstorming Techniques on Risk Identification

Brainstorming is one of the most common types of informal idea invention. It comes in handy in many situations where creative, cognitive thinking is required. In real world, there's a significant amount of brainstormers who are asked to solve simple problems, like come up with creative uses for a cup. When using brainstorming technique to make risk analysis, things can be quite different; mostly because the problems (and solutions) are often complex and critical to the success of the participants. The following are useful tips for effectively brainstorming.

1. Prepare the "Homework"

Before the brainstorming session, think carefully about the real problem and goals to be achieved. Perhaps the most important part of homework is to ask participants to prepare. They need to understand the problem and brainstorming process ahead of time. Before the meeting, send out homework that describes the process and encourages participants to start researching the problem, and also to come to the meeting with a list of ideas.

2. Choose a Brainstorming Facilitator

Facilitator is the person who guides and hosts the brainstorming session. A productive brainstorming session need not just a facilitator, but a creative thinking facilitator; not just any facilitator, but a brainstorming facilitator who is sophistic with how to cut off criticism, ensure full participation, and keep the team on track.

Every person needs to feel comfortable and encouraged to present ideas. You don't want participants to be concerned about saying or doing something wrong in front of the boss. The boss can introduce the session but should only return at the end of the process — when he or she is asked to make implementation decisions.

However, creative thinking facilitation is a skill that takes months or years to master. Good facilitators can nurture creativity by using thinking tools. For example, creativity can be inspired by guiding the team to think about individual characteristics of the problem one at a time or by using tools such as reversed assumptions, random words, or a morphological matrix.

3. Suspend Judgment

This is the area where many brainstorming procedures go wrong. The facilitator or the other participants tend to habitually evaluate ideas, which is counterproductive during idea generation. A critical principle of brainstorming is postponing judgment. For example, "We don't have budget for that." Or: "There's no way a resource would be approved for that." Or: "We've tried that before and it didn't work." And so on. A popular metaphor used to describe that type of team problem solving is "driving with the brakes on." Allowing judgment during brainstorming isn't effective for idea generation. Even "bad ideas" could be the fertilizer out of which good ideas grow.

The object of brainstorming is to get as many of ideas on the table as possible in a limited time. There will be plenty of time later to sort through the ideas and decide which are worth pursuing. Therefore, the quantity of ideas generated should be emphasized in the first place.

4. Choose A Small Diverse Group of Participants

Another important factor that heavily influences the outcome of brainstorming is the exact mix of participants. It's important to keep the size of the group workable. If the team is dysfunctional, smaller groups may work better, about 4-7 people. However, if the team is highly functional, it could possibly go up to 12 people. The increasing number of participants is tended to encourage social loafing. Be sure participants have diverse backgrounds and experiences. In the book, *How Breakthroughs Happen*, Hargadon argues that innovation occurs when isolated groups integrate previously unrelated viewpoints and technologies to resolve new problems.

Last but not least, it's very important to remember that brainstorming is not a panacea. It's only the first step in a longer process. After the ideas are generated, other tools and techniques are necessary to evaluate and implement ideas. And very importantly, the culture of the organization needs to be conducive and supportive of the entire creative process. After ideas are generated, teams still need rapid decision making and support in order to create truly innovative solutions.

(Adapted from: Marshall, Lisa B. "How to Brainstorm")

After identifying the crises with brainstorming, it is necessary to analyze and evaluate the crises. "Probability-Severity Matrix" is a very effective tool to categorize crises that have been identified (See Table 10.2).

运用头脑风暴进行危机识别后，可以使用"可能性—严重性矩阵"对识别出的危机进行评估。

Table 10.2 Probability-Severity Matrix
表 10.2 可能性—严重性矩阵

Probability	Severity				
	Insignificant	Minor	Moderate	Significant	Catastrophic
Certain	MEDIUM	HIGH	EXTREME	EXTREME	EXTREME
Likely	MEDIUM	HIGH	HIGH	EXTREME	EXTREME
Possible	LOW	MEDIUM	HIGH	EXTREME	EXTREME
Unlikely	LOW	LOW	MEDIUM	HIGH	EXTREME
Remote	LOW	LOW	MEDIUM	HIGH	HIGH

The vectors of the matrix are probability and severity respectively. In vertical side, the probability of crisis can be scaled as certain, likely, possible, unlikely and remote; while in horizontal side, the severity of crisis can be scaled as insignificant, minor, moderate, significant and catastrophic. According to the criteria of the matrix, all crises can be classified as low risk, medium risk, high risk and extreme risk. Crisis communication plans could be developed according to different risk levels.

(2) Drafting a communication plan.

In business when a crisis breaks out, the organization need to consider how to communicate with the public and what information to share.

可能性—严重性矩阵的向量分别为可能性和严重性。根据可能性与严重性的程度，将风险分为低风险、中等风险、高风险和极高风险四个等级。针对不同的风险等级设计危机沟通方案。

（2）制定沟通计划。

当危机爆发时，组织需要考虑如何与公众沟通以及如何发布信息。信息不准确

Reporting inaccurate information can negatively affect your reputation for trustworthiness and stability. Allowing false rumors to flourish also has a negative effect. Therefore, a crisis communication plan needs to be prepared in advance. In this plan, a representative who speaks on behalf of the organization to the media will be appointed. Pre-script answers or outlines to common questions should be prepared.

(3) Organizing crisis communication group.

Brainstorm to form a group of people as crisis communication team for the organization, who will be in responsible for drafting the crisis communication plan. Several roles need to be filled in crisis management process:

① Spokesperson — the only one who speaks to the media.

② Commander / coordinator — who coordinates all responses to the crisis.

③ Liaisons for each of your audiences — who answers calls and provide scripted information to audiences.

④ Media coverage collector — who gather all coverage of the event on each communication channels, such as television, in the newspaper, and on the web.

⑤ Press release and speech writer.

The crisis communication group should have a specific venue as for work station. In an emergency, the communication group would gather to have meetings, coordinate response to audience requests, hold a press conference if necessary, and also do other tasks.

或任由谣言散布会对组织的信誉和稳定性产生负面影响。因此，需要提前制定危机沟通计划，包括任命媒体发言人并准备好常见问题的回复提纲。

（3）组建危机沟通团队。

通过头脑风暴组建组织的危机沟通团队，负责起草危机沟通计划。危机管理过程中需要几个角色：

① 发言人：唯一对媒体发言的人。

② 指挥者/协调者：协调所有危机应对行动。

③ 联络官：接听受众的电话，并向其提供文字信息。

④ 媒体报道收集人：汇集各种媒体对危机事件的所有报道。

⑤ 召开新闻发布会，起草发言通稿。

危机沟通小组应有明确的工作地点。在紧急情况下，沟通小组将召集会议，协调对观众请求的响应，召开新闻发布会，并执行其他任务。

During a crisis, the place should be available on short notice. It is also important that the place is in good condition with cellphone signals, telephone lines, Internet connection, and other technology to sustain communication.

(4) Defining the audiences in a crisis.

Every organization has certain audiences it needs to communicate with, both internal and external. Generally, during a crisis, the audiences need to be paid attention to including:

① Employees — the communication with full-time employees, part time employees, and freelancers should be differently organized.

② Media — Since the news media reaches a wide audience, you'll want to include them as a constituency.

③ Customers, or anyone who uses your products or services.

④ Government officials or regulators.

⑤ Other Stakeholders, such as the suppliers, the public, the stock holders, etc.

Unlike other audiences, the news media can influence the public at large through their coverage.

Consider the following questions on how to keep the media updated with the latest developments.

① Who will be responsible for briefing the media on extended crises?

② Is it necessary to create a news media briefing center to facilitate communication?

③ How to access the reporters into organization or crisis on site? Generally,

发生危机后，危机沟通小组的工作地点应即时发布，并确保通信设备与技术状况良好。

（4）确定危机沟通对象。

不同的组织有不同的内外部沟通对象，在危机沟通中常常包括以下几种：

① 雇员。与全职、兼职、灵活用工人员的沟通应加以区别。

② 媒体。由于媒体可以接触不同受众，你会想把他们都作为支持者。

③ 客户或者使用你的产品或服务的人。

④ 政府官员。

⑤ 其他利益相关者，如供应商、公众、股东等。

相较于与其他听众，新闻媒体可以通过其报道影响大众。可以通过考虑一些问题来让媒体随时了解最新进展。

shutting the media out entirely could result in negative coverage.

④ How to assure factual information is given out by official spokesperson?

⑤ How to react to other source of information?

The contact information for each group of audiences should be compiled in advance, since you don't want to be searching for contact information during an emergency. So, get prepared for the name of contact person, business telephone number, mobile number, email address, social media account, etc.

(5) Scripting responses to crises.

Each audience will have different questions based on how the incident may affect them. Consider about common questions and draft template answers to use during the crisis.

① Employees: "Should I report to work? When?" "Is it safe to return to work?" "Will I be paid during the shutdown?" "What happened to my coworker?"

② News media: "What happened?" "Who caused the incident?" "Were there injuries or fatalities?" "Who is responsible for this?" "What's your plan for keeping this incident from happening again?"

③ Customers: "When will my product arrive?" "Will you compensate me for the inconvenience?"

④ Government officials and regulators: "What happened and when?" "How is the public impacted?" "When will you be back in service?" "How many employees

为了便于紧急联系，应提前收集各类听众的联系方式，例如联系人姓名、公司电话、手机、电子邮件、社交媒体账户等。

（5）制定危机应答草案。

根据事件对自身的影响，每类听众都会有不同的问题。应考虑常见问题并起草危机期间的标准应答。

are affected by this?"

After identifying the questions, you should write out answers and include blank lines for information that will change. These templates will be helpful during a crisis. Avoid using "no comments" as an answer in crisis communication. For issues that are under investigation, let the audience know you will get back to them when you have further information. For issues that relate to personal or legal matters, explain patiently that confidential information could not be leaked out.

Admitting responsibility is also a good answer in crisis communication. The public is forgiving if the communicator is willing to admit mistakes and take responsibilities.

(6) Completing the crisis communication plan.

In order to confirm the challenges and opportunities have not been ignored, the organization is recommended to have a practice drill and run through the communication plan. When the test has been completed, convene the crisis communication group to identify any weaknesses. The communication plan sometimes become outdated. Contact information for team members need to be updated periodically.

Distribute the communication plan, and make sure key personnel receive a copy of the plan. Make it available in printed form and in electronic format. Remind people that the communication plan should not be distributed to unauthorized personnel.

2. In-Crisis

Under the circumstance of solving organization

尽量提前思考各类问题的回复方案。避免使用"无可奉告"作为答案,对于正在调查的问题,可以告知听众将及时回复最新进展,对于涉及私人或法律事务的问题,应告知其因故不可能泄露。

在危机沟通中,承认责任也是一个很好的答案。如果传播者愿意承认错误并承担责任,将会取得公众的谅解。

(6)完善危机沟通计划。

为了确保危机沟通计划的完整性,建议对整个计划进行演练,并及时完善。根据需要定期更新危机沟通计划,如联系信息。

可以以印刷形式和电子形式向关键人员下发沟通计划。并提醒人们未经授权不得转发。

2. 危机中

在危机中的处理与控制

or enterprise crisis, in-crisis control is usually viewed as the key point. Although full preparation and no crisis is expected by all organizations, the actual aim normally falls on saving reputation, reducing loss and avoiding negative effect expanded when crisis takes place. In this situation, efficient communication takes the part of flowing blood in an emergency surgery to keep vitality.

至关重要。组织进行危机中的干预以挽回声誉、减少损失，并尽量避免危机的负面影响。在这个过程中需要进行有效沟通。

Crisis communication tactics during the crisis stage may include the following: the development of a crisis management team; the collection and processing of pertinent information to the crisis management team for decision making; and the dissemination of crisis messages to both internal and external publics of the organization.

危机发生阶段的沟通策略包括：成立危机处理小组；收集和处理相关信息，供危机管理团队决策；以及确定向组织内外部公众传达的危机信息。

Since the attention of public opinion is a significant feature of crisis, communication with media can not be neglected in crisis. To control the public voice, the organization or the enterprise need to fully understand the role of media and master the rules of crisis communication with media. Crisis management expert M. Regester. Michael make a point in his book *Crisis Management* that when handling a crisis, take the control over providing information is quite important and proposed "3T Theory".

公众舆论的关注性是危机事件的特征之一，组织或企业需要充分理解媒体的作用并掌握与媒体进行危机沟通的方法才能有效地控制舆论。

3T Theory
(1) Tell your own tale: provide information proactively.
Proactive actions can help reduce or prevent information interference from other channel to ensure the authority, authenticity and reliability of information.

Furthermore, the content of information can be controlled and adjusted under the specific situation of the crisis.

(2) Tell it all: tell all the information related to the crisis and the information must be true.

After the crisis, there will be a lot of speculative remarks on the media platform. If the senior executives know the crisis situation much later than the media, the crisis management can be very difficult. Regardless of the extent to which the company understands the fact, the spokesperson needs to provide all the facts he or she understands and emphasize the facts and opinions confirmed. When the information in hand is limited, the stand and attitude, the confidence of handling the crisis and actions taken can all be provided to media.

(3) Tell it fast: react fast and update the crisis-related information.

Once crisis break out, it will immediately become the focus of public attention. The faster you move, the more controllable the crisis will be. Nowadays, with the rapid development of Internet and social media, the speed of information dissemination is faster and the breadth is wider, thus need more timely reaction.

3T法则：以我为主提供情况：牢牢掌握信息发布主动权；提供全部情况：信息发布全面、真实，而且必须实言相告；尽快提供情况：危机处理时应该尽快不断地发布信息。

(Adapted from: Michael Regester. Crisis Management[M]. Random House Business Books, 1989)

Facing reality and taking actions sometimes are difficult and painful. However, in crisis communication, instead of being ostriches who dig their heads into the sand and think they can't see anything or have nothing to do with anything, enterprises should communicate with active, rapid and decisive eagle strategy. Crisis control measures including recalling products, compensating relevant personnel, using authoritative opinions, using legal means

在危机沟通中，企业应该敢于积极应对问题，做善于观察主动出击的雄鹰而不是逃避现实的鸵鸟。应尽快采取危机管理措施，包括召回产品，补偿相关人员，听取专家意见，采取法律措施，通过媒体重塑公众形象等。

and shaping the public image through the media should be carried out timely.

3. Post-Crisis

Crisis is not necessarily a bad thing. It may be a radical change for good as well as bad. After pre-crisis and in-crisis actions, effective post-crisis tactics will help transfer crisis into an experience with profound influence.

Provide for an After-Action Report (AAR). As part of continually improving your crisis communication plan, you should convene meetings of your crisis communications team after an incident. Include a provision for creating an AAR.

3. 危机后

危机同时可意味着一种转机。合理的危机后沟通技巧将有利于将危机转化为具有长远有益影响的经验。

提供行动后报告（AAR）。作为持续改进危机沟通计划的一部分，应在事件发生后召集危机沟通团队会议，创建AAR指导原则。

Example:

"Within 10 days of the crisis or incident, the team will convene to review any lessons learned. These lessons will be included in an AAR, which can then form the basis of a more comprehensive AAR to be shared with management."

There are several key issues for post crisis communication including information disclosure, reputation repair and the discourse of renewal.

In post crisis phase, a comprehensive crisis report is the commonly used. A final crisis report should cover such essential information as the brief of crisis, the cause, developments and current situation of the crisis, the actions taken, effects and future plan of crisis management, etc. The emphasis of the crisis report for internal communication need to be put on the information

危机后沟通的重要内容包括信息披露、声誉修复、后续改进。

危机后信息披露的重要内容是详细的危机报告，具体内容应包括危机原因、过程、当前情况、采取何手段、危机管理的未来措施等简况。危机后的内部沟通应包括股东关心的损失报告、恢复措施等问题；外部沟通应把公

that the stakeholders care about like the damage analysis and recovery measures, while the external crisis report should take public reaction into account, which means to think about public emotion and guide their responses and opinions about the crisis result. In most cases, the coherence between these two reports is very important. Information conflicts in the reports may lead to another reputation crisis which may cause the collapse of trust.

In the post crisis stage, repairing reputation gradually will become a prior subject. It is a process that starts from in-crisis communication but need to be highlight in the post-crisis communication. Based on the different situations of the crisis and the strategies taken in the previous communication process, repair strategies can be mainly classified into the following types: attack the accuser, denial, excuse, scapegoat, compensation and apology.

The repair strategies of attacking the accuser, denial, excuse and scapegoat are more taken by those organizations meet with victim cluster crisis. Attacking the accuser is to confront the person or group who disclose the incident. Denial is the guidelines of asserting that there is no crisis. If the crisis manager takes the scapegoat strategy, the core of whole crisis communication is to blame the person or group outside of the organization. Excuse is the strategy of denying intent to do harm as well as minimizing organizational responsibility.

To the public, compensation and apologies

众反映考虑在内，对公众情感和反应进行有效引导。分别针对内外部的危机报告对于危机后信任的建立都非常重要。

后危机管理中，信誉的修复非常重要。延续前期危机沟通的过程，信誉修复的策略包括：攻击原告，否认，借口，寻找"替罪羊"，补偿和道歉。

攻击原告，否认，借口，寻找"替罪羊"四种策略常常被用在组织自身也是受害者的危机中。

对于公众而言，及时的

are usually the best way to save the reputation which shows the responsible attitude of the organization or the company.

The apology needs to be authentic and sincere, properly admitting the mistakes made in the current situation and finding a good starting point to ask stakeholders, victims and public for forgiveness. Compensation on the other hand is often related with the victims in the crisis by organization or the company offering money or other gifts. With the actual help given to the victims, the public can see the action of the organization while reputation concerns are addressed.

The disclosure of renewal shows the intention to change and never make the same mistake which covers the contents of the future plan of correcting the past mistake and the measures taken to add promise to the related possible problems.

补偿和道歉是恢复声誉、重建信任的最佳做法。

道歉应该诚恳，恰当的承认失误，并争取股东、受害者和公众的谅解。补偿是指对受害者的物质补偿或其他形式的补偿，让受害者得到真切的帮助，公众可以看到组织为了重建声誉而作出的努力。

改进措施表达了组织对过去发生错误的反思，并积极采取措施避免未来发生类似事件。

Mini Case: Muji Crisis Management

In 2017, After being accused of selling food produced in nuclear contaminated area by the TV program, Muji quickly get to know the situation and made post-crisis announcement. The announcement first pointed out the misunderstanding between origin address and register address and then claimed the real origin area of the two products accused. In the last part, Muji made a very convincing claim with law and regulations, providing official documents and promised their attitude to provide trustworthy products to customers. The whole researching and announcement process only took less than 20 hours. The fast and accurate disclosure of information and renewal leave the public with a sincere and reliable image of Muji and turns the crisis into an opportunity to show their credit.

【Conclusion】本章小结

Crisis is an or a series of specific, unexpected and non-routine organizationally based events that creates high levels of uncertainty and threat or perceived threat to an organization. It can be divided into three types of crises including the victim cluster, the accidental cluster and the intentional cluster.

In crisis communication, main communication groups can be divided into internal and external targets.

Communication is an important part of crisis management. crisis communication strategies are discussed according to the process of pre-crisis, in-crisis and post-crisis stages.

【Case Study】案例讨论

Fifteen people dead, 70 injured, a frightened community, and a $1 per barrel increase in oil prices. British Petroleum (BP) faced these public relations obstacles and more following the March 23, 2005 refinery explosion in Texas City, Texas. The oil refinery explosion was a human breakdown crisis that challenged the organization and its crisis response personnel.

The explosion occurred at approximately 1:20 p.m. at British Petroleum's isomerization unit. According to Moran (2005: 4), the blast rattled homes as far as 5 miles away and covered the skies in ash and debris at the refinery complex located off of Texas 146. A news report (Aulds et al., 2005), and an alert summary provided by the NC4 Incident Monitoring Center (2005), indicated the massive plume of black smoke sent into the air by the explosion prompted Texas City Emergency Management to issue a shelter-in-place order for the city and declared the explosion a level 3 alert at 1:28 p.m. At 2:10 p.m. the city lifted the shelter-in-place order and reduced the alert to a level 2. Approximately five minutes later, city first responder units called for backup and additional ambulances from across the county. At 3:22 p.m. British Petroleum fire crews doused the fire and by 3:30 p.m. the rescue and recovery mission began. During this time period, the Texas Department of Transportation temporarily closed all eastbound lanes of FM 1764 and FM 519 entering Texas City. In addition, local school facilities were locked down and several nearby buildings and vehicles were damaged by the explosion. By 7 p.m., British Petroleum officials had confirmed at least 14 dead and more than 70 company employees injured, but cautioned that both totals could rise. Additionally, one oil refinery worker had not been accounted for by 7:18 p.m.

In a letter to refinery employees written by Don Parus and released at 10:16 p.m. (CT) on the day of the explosion, ingratiation and excuse are embedded in the expression of sorrow for the loss and injury of workers. Parus (2005a) wrote: "We have made strides in safety and felt we were making progress. These events must remind us that whatever we have done it is just not enough."

The crisis management plan (CMP) was initiated by British Petroleum as early as six hours after the explosion occurred. By 7:10 p.m., phone numbers were released for family members to call to retrieve information about the explosion and their loved ones. A property claims number was also released for those community members whose property was damaged by the explosion. Support personnel were made available to provide assistance to the victims' relatives and hotel accommodations were provided for families who had traveled to the area. By the following day, British Petroleum had set up a website (www.bpresponse.org) to relay information about the explosion to community members and other stakeholders. This website boosted British Petroleum's availability to stakeholders through the inclusion of press releases, incident fact sheets, videos and, most importantly, a questions/comments form where inquiries about specific information concerning the explosion could be answered by British Petroleum spokesperson Hugh Depland.

Corrective action is illustrated in a BP America (2005) release detailing the steps taken to reinforce safety and prevent similar incidents from occurring. The actions include a review of every unit's safety protection system, a relocation of personnel from trailers within 500 feet of blowdown stacks and flares, relocation of those whose jobs do not require them to be near refinery equipment, improved internal emergency communication, and a review of all safety emergency systems.

In addition, Pillari (2005b) states, "We can assure that those who were injured and the families of those who died receive financial support and compensation. Our goal is to provide fair compensation without the need for lawsuits or lengthy court proceedings." Pillari goes on to discuss how British Petroleum has begun contacting families and is attempting to expedite and simplify the settlement process. Therefore,

Pillari publicly stated the organization took full responsibility for the explosion and asked forgiveness, while providing compensation to restore the public's image of British Petroleum. In the aforementioned statement made by Pillari, corrective action is appropriate, as causes for the explosion were determined and could have been prevented.

(Adapted from: Michelle Maresh and David E. Williams. "Oil Industry Crisis Communication")

Questions:
(1) What crisis communication actions did British Petroleum take immediately after the crisis break out?
(2) In post-crisis state, what did British Petroleum do to make crisis communication with different groups (employees, the public, stakeholders, etc.)?
(3) Find another example of oil industry crisis and compare the crisis communication actions.

【Study Questions】课后问题

1. What are the types of crisis?
2. What are the requirements of communicating with internal staff in crisis?
3. What are crisis communication tactics in the pre-crisis, in-crisis and post-crisis stages?

Chapter 11　Cross-Cultural Communication

第11章　跨文化沟通

With the further development of globalization and the strengthened ties among countries, our globe has become a virtual "global village". The companies around the world are also under such great influences, which can be both opportunities and challenges. Therefore, cross-cultural communication becomes a critical issue in nowadays business communication.

In this chapter, you will learn:
- the different dimensions of culture;
- the skills and strategies in cross-cultural communication.

随着全球化的进一步深化和各国之间联系的不断加强,世界各地的公司都面临全球化的机遇和挑战。在全球化背景下的商务沟通中,跨文化沟通占据重要位置。

本章将学习文化的不同维度以及跨文化沟通当中的技巧与策略。

11.1　The Dimensions of Culture

一、文化维度理论

One most influential theory of culture dimensions is proposed by Holland scholar Hofstede. In his theories, Hofstede lists five most important dimensions of culture, namely: individualism vs. collectivism, uncertainty avoidance, power distance, masculinity/femininity, and long-term vs. short-term orientation.

荷兰管理学者霍夫斯泰德提出的文化维度理论至今仍具有巨大影响力。在该理论中,霍夫斯泰德列举了五种最为重要的文化维度。

1. Individualism vs. Collectivism

1. 个人主义/集体主义

The difference between collectivism and individualism is in what each ideology considers

个人主义和集体主义最大的区别在于在认知上个人

as important: the individual or the group.

In collectivism, it is some sort of group rather than an individual who is at the center of all social, political, and economic concerns, and issues. Those who are proponents of this ideology say that the interests and claims of groups (it may even be a state) supersede those of individuals. Thus, a society being a group is considered to be superior to an individual.

Collectivism believes in the subjugation of the individual to a group, which may be family, tribe, society, party or a state. Individual has to sacrifice for the collective good of the people. The proponents of collectivism consider their stand to be superior to those of individualists as they are morally superior thinking of the collective good of the group or the society.

Individualism focuses on the individual. It is not that an individual is any different from the society. However, an individualist, even while remaining within the society thinks about personal interests. This doctrine believes that society is there, but it is ultimately made up of individuals who choose and act. The foundation of individualism lies in one's moral right, to pursue one's own happiness. However, it is not in contradiction with collectivism as it believes that it is necessary for individuals to preserve and defend institutions that have been made to protect one's right to pursue happiness.

Individualists rely on their own efforts to defend their interests and put emphasis on

还是集体更重要。

在集体主义视角下，集体而非个人是整个社会、政治、经济事务的核心。

集体利益包括家庭、族群、社会、党派或是国家的利益；集体主义观认为个人利益应服从于集体利益，具有道德上的优越性。

个人主义者认为，社会是由个人组成的。个人主义的基础在于人的道德权利，追求自己的幸福。然而，在这一点上，个体主义者并不与集体主义相矛盾，因为集体主义也认为个人有必要保护和捍卫为保护自己追求幸福的权利而建立的制度。

个人主义者依靠个人努力为自己谋取利益，重视自

their own value, while collectivists rely on the organizations to defend their interests, in the meantime remain absolute loyal to their organizations; the core value of individualism is the freedom and independence of individuals, while the core value of collectivism is the harmony of the group/organization; the main differentiation in individualism is oneself or others, while that of collectivism is to join or to break away from an organization. Therefore, during communication, the key point in individualism is to present a distinct point of view, while that of collectivism is to put emphasis on relationships rather than tasks.

In terms of countries and nations, some countries are more inclined to individualism, such as America, Britain, Canada, Australia, etc. In these countries, organizations respect individual choices, employees can defend their own self-interests, and their corporate cultures would put more emphasis on individual initiatives.

In contrast, in some more collectivism-oriented countries, such as Mexico, Greece, Colombia, etc., the organizations there are more like "families", and would defend employees' interests. In return, the organizations would demand the employees' loyalty, sense of duty and group participation.

As a result, while communicating with people from different cultural background, you should take this aspect of their culture into consideration and make communication strategies accordingly.

身的价值，强调的是个体的自由和独立，在交流当中强调观点鲜明，而集体主义者依附结合紧密的社会型组织，并对组织绝对忠诚，要求的是团队的和谐，并认为关系比任务更重要。

偏向于个人主义的国家如美、英、加、澳大利亚等，组织尊重个人选择，员工更关注个人兴趣，企业文化强调个体参与、进取与首创精神。

而与之相对，偏向于集体主义的国家，如墨西哥、希腊、日本、哥伦比亚等，组织更像是"家庭"来影响员工的兴趣，企业文化更多强调的则是群体参与、忠诚与责任感。

因此，跨文化沟通策略应考虑该国文化背景从而制定相应的沟通内容和策略。

2. Uncertainty Avoidance

Uncertainty avoidance, which reflects if an organization use formal ways such as rules, strategies and institutions to reduce exposure to an uncertain future. The core value of uncertainty avoidance is clearance, as its key point "it is dangerous to allow deviations", the prior question in such a culture is "right or wrong". In contrast, in uncertainty-tolerant culture, the core values are exploration and questing, as it believes that "difference brings curiosity", therefore the prior question in such a culture is "urgent or not".

In culture featured with strong uncertainty avoidance, it tends to build up more work regulations, procedures and rules to deal with uncertainties. Generally, peremptory norms lead to pressure in working place. In contrast, culture with weak uncertainty avoidance emphasizes less on control and standardization. The environment in such society and work place tends to encourage relaxed and diversified attitude (See Table 11.1).

2. 不确定性规避

不确定性规避是指组织用规则、战略、制度等正式渠道来规避和控制不确定性。不确定性规避的文化倾向回避"不确定",认为存在偏差是危险的,因而"是非判断"非常重要;而不确定性包容的文化,其核心价值观是"搜索、探寻",相信差异带来好奇,因而对问题紧迫性的判断非常重要。

在不确定性规避较强的文化中,倾向建立更多的工作条例、流程或规范以应付不确定性,强制性规范使工作环境富有压力感;在不确定性规避弱的文化中,会较少强调控制,因此标准化程度较低,而更倾向于放松和多样化的态度倾向。

Table 11.1　Traits of Uncertainty Avoidance
表11.1　不确定性规避的特征

	High Uncertainty Avoidance	Low Uncertainty Avoidance
Social norms	conservatism, law and order	openness to change, innovation
	xenophobic	tolerance of diversity
	express emotions	suppress emotions
Politics/legal system	weak interest in politics	high interest in politics

(To be continued)

(Continue)

	High Uncertainty Avoidance	**Low Uncertainty Avoidance**
Politics/legal system	citizen protest repressed	citizen protest accepted
	more and specific laws and regulations	fewer and general laws and regulations
religion	Catholic, Islam, Judaism, Shintoism aggressively fundamentalist ritualized/ceremonial	Protestant, Buddhism, Taoism, Hinduism little persecution for beliefs avoid ritualization and ceremony
school	teachers have all answers	teachers may say "don't know"
	structured learning	open-ended learning
family	traditional gender roles	fewer gender roles
	children taught world is hostile	children taught world is benevolent

In the countries that have low uncertainty avoidance, such as the US, UK, Sweden and Denmark, the companies have less structuring of activities and fewer written rules; instead, they have greater variability and greater willingness to take risks. On the contrary, in countries that have high uncertainty avoidance such as China, Japan, France, Greece, Portugal, etc., the companies have more structuring of activities and written rules, therefore more standardization and less willingness to take risks.

3. Power Distance

Are you nervous in front of your boss?

Dare you propose opposite opinions against your boss face to face?

These questions reflect another aspect of cultural dimension: power distance. It indicates

不确定规避较弱的国家如美、英、瑞典和丹麦，企业的结构性活动和明文规定较少，企业文化崇尚多样化和冒险；不确定性规避较强的国家如中国、日本、法国、希腊、葡萄牙等，企业的结构性活动和明文规定较多，企业文化更崇尚标准化和安全性。

3. 权力距离

你在领导面前是否很紧张？是否敢向老板提出不同意见？

权力距离指人们对权力差距的接受程度以及对权力

how people tolerate power imbalance and how people respect those of power. In high-power-distance cultures, social status is highly esteemed, and the prior difference in such a culture is power vs. dependence. On the contrary, in low-power-distance culture, social status is not so highly valued, and people are considered equal, therefore the prior issue is to take full responsibility for work.

When reflected in business, the companies with high-power-distance culture tend to choose formal hierarchical organizational structures, and decision-making processes are often from top downward; while in companies with low-power-distance cultures, corporate organizational structures are relatively flat, and decision-making processes are often from the bottom upward or two-ways.

In terms of countries, those more inclined to high power distance would include Mexico, India, Brazil, Philippines, China, etc. In these countries, pyramid organizational structures are popular with greater centralization and more supervisory personnel. Also, white-collar jobs are higher valued comparing with blue collar jobs in these countries. In contrast, other countries with low power distance, such as Austria, Denmark, Sweden, Norway, etc., the corporations have less centralization and flatter organization pyramids, therefore fewer supervisory personnel, and manual and clerical work are equally valued.

4. Masculinity vs. Femininity

This dimension determines whether an

的尊重程度。权力距离较大的文化中，尊崇社会地位，社会的主要差异在于强权与依附；在权力距离较小的文化里，人们信奉"人人平等"，社会的主要差异则在于对事、对人负责，社会结构趋于分权。

在权力距离较大的企业文化中，企业的组织结构比较陡峭，趋向于采用自上而下的决策方式；在权力距离较小的企业文化中，企业的组织结构则比较扁平，更趋向于自下而上或双向决策方式。

权力距离较大的国家如墨西哥、印度、巴西、菲律宾等，企业制度趋于集权，组织结构呈现为金字塔形且监督者多，白领工作被视为比蓝领工作更有价值；权力距离较小的国家如奥地利、丹麦、瑞典和挪威，企业制度趋于分权及扁平化管理，监督者较少，而蓝领工作与白领工作所受到的尊重并无差别。

4. 男性主义/女性主义

男性主义与女性主义维

organization is more assertive or more cooperative, as masculinity usually represents competitiveness and aggressiveness, while femininity usually represents modesty and affection, etc.

In masculine culture, the core value is to pursue success and power. There is significant difference between men and women; while in a feminine culture, the core value is to care about others, and the main difference is to love or to be loved. As a result, a masculine society tends to be confident, self-assured and aggressive. People in such a society are candid and persistent about pursuing money. In contrast, a feminine society tends to be friendly and modest, the job positions in such a society are relatively stable, and team work is highly valued.

In terms of countries, more feminine countries include Sweden, Denmark, Thailand, etc. In these countries, gender roles are minimized, and soft, intuitive skills are rewarded. Also, in these countries, there are more women in jobs with high social status; In contrast, the countries that are more masculine include Japan, Austria, Italy, Mexico, etc. In these countries, gender roles are differentiated, and aggression, competition, justice are rewarded. Also, in these countries, there are fewer women in jobs with high social status.

5. Long-term/Short-term Orientation Dimension

The long-term/short-term orientation dimension refers to how people could tolerate the delay on satisfaction of their material, emotional,

度主要看某一社会代表男性的品质如竞争性、独断性更多，还是代表女性的品质如谦虚、关爱他人更多。

男性主义文化中，核心价值观是争强好胜；在女性主义文化中，核心价值观是关爱他人，角色差别是关爱与被关爱。男性主义文化的社会趋于自信武断，进取好胜，崇尚赚钱；女性主义文化的社会则偏向友好柔和，职位安全和团队合作。

更具女性主义特征的国家如瑞典、丹麦、泰国等，性别角色差异弱化，女性承担较重工作，重视柔性、直觉能力等特征；更具男性主义特征的国家如日本、奥地利、意大利、墨西哥等，性别角色区分清晰，女性较少承担重要工作，社会文化更强调斗志、竞争性和公正等男性特质。

5. 长期导向/短期导向维度

长期导向和短期导向维度指对物质、情感、社会需求的延迟满足接受度。该维

and social needs. This dimension is based on the philosophy of Confucius and has to do with persistence, thrift, personal stability and respect for tradition.

In long-term orientation culture, people focus on long-term interests, thrift and saving; while in a short-term orientation culture, people focus on the present and tend to seek short-term efficiency.

As a result of such differences, people in different countries could take different approaches in negotiations.

When negotiate with Chinese, they would start with plant visiting, inspection trip and other business activities, in the meanwhile, observe whether the influential partner is trustworthy enough to establish long term relationship.

When negotiating with Americans, they would expect the influential partner to focus on the present deal and be straight-forward, so as to close the deal as soon as possible.

In real-life communication, the above five dimensions usually mix and overlap, as this has close relationship with the integration and blending of cultures. As a result, while applying these five dimensions to real-life communication, you are supposed to be flexible in accordance to different situations.

11.2 Skills and Techniques of Cross-Cultural Communication

Be aware of the dimensions of culture is

度基于儒家学说衍生而来，强调坚韧、节俭、个人稳定和对传统的尊重等品质。

长期导向的文化中，人们聚焦于长远利益，崇尚节俭和储蓄；短期导向的文化中，人们关注短期成效。

不同的商务谈判方法是一个很好的例子。

中国人商务谈判时会先进行工厂参观考察等商务活动，同时观察对方是否值得信任，以期建立长期合作关系。

当与美国人谈判的时候，他们会希望聚焦于眼前的生意，开门见山，就事论事，且希望能尽快达成协议。

在现实交流中，这五个维度往往交叉融合，这也和文化的一体性和交融性有着密切的关系，因此在应用的时候也要灵活变通，不可拘泥。

二、跨文化沟通技巧

在理解文化差异的重要

critical, however, cross-culture differences can be tough to navigate. The communicator should grasp some skills and techniques to make cross-cultural communications successful.

1. Adopting a Flexible Attitude

To build good relationships with people from other cultures, it is essential to learn how to communicate with them. Sometimes, while communicating with people with different cultural background, we tend to judge other people's behavior according to our own cultural values, which would lead to severe obstacles for smooth communication.

People from different cultures have different verbal and non-verbal communication patterns. For example, they will speak at different volumes, be more or less direct in showing emotion, may or may not expect to engage in "small talk," and exhibit other dissimilarities in communication. When communicating with people from other cultures, be prepared to encounter such differences, including ones that you were not aware of.

To be a successful communicator, you will also need to pay attention to the unwritten rules about social hierarchy in face-to-face communication. For instance, you may come from a culture where men and women are expected to communicate equally with each other, but your counterparty could come from a culture where men may do more talking. Similarly, you may be communicating with someone who expects that a younger person should let an older person do most

性基础上，应掌握必要的跨文化沟通技巧。

1. 采取灵活的态度

与来自不同文化背景的人打交道，应懂得如何去沟通。以自我文化观念、价值观、道德作标准衡量他人的行为，将会对沟通造成一定的障碍。

不同文化中，沟通的语言和非语言习惯不同。例如，交谈的音量、会否愿意直接表达情感，会否愿意"闲聊"，或标新立异。交流时，要准备好面对这些差异，包括那些你不知道的差异。

在面对面的交流中，要注意不同文化下的社会地位差异。比如有的文化中男女交流地位平等，而有的文化倾向于男士占交流的主导地位，有的文化倾向长者主导交流，而有的希望不同年龄的人能够平等交流。

of the talking, while you expect people across age groups to communicate equally.

Cultural hegemonism is one of the greatest hinders in cross-cultural communicating. While having cross-cultural communication, the two parties sometimes do not have equal positions. Some circumstances happen occasionally. For example, if the dominant party impose its own set of cultural norms on the weaker side and forcefully ask the weaker party to follow, the inferiority complex of the weaker party could be initiated to some extent, and cause negative response in communication. Each culture has its own set of dominant values, beliefs, and prejudices. Even if cultural differences come up explicitly in conversation, be tolerant and open-minded instead of argumentative.

文化霸权主义是跨文化沟通中最大的障碍之一。跨文化沟通中的双方地位往往不平等。强势者易将自己的文化准则强加于弱势者，并强行要求对方遵循，进而可能引发劣势者的文化自卑感，而消极应对沟通，不能实现顺畅的交流。

每种文化都有独特的价值观、信仰、成见。在跨文化沟通中应保持容忍和开放。

2. Avoid Verbal Offenses

In cross-cultural communication, language is the primary tool, and different languages embody different cultural backgrounds. Even the same words may have different meanings under different circumstances or even voice tones (which is especially true for the Chinese language), let alone the confusion caused by words with the same sound but different meanings. It is rather difficult for professional interpreters to translate the subtle tones of words, let alone those of us who aren't professionals of languages. Therefore, while communicating cross-culturally, be careful with the words you choose, and do

2. 避免语言冒犯

语言是跨文化沟通的首要工具。不同语言有着不同的深厚文化背景。同样的表达在不同的场合甚至不同声调下的意思相差甚远。专业翻译做到准确也相当困难，更何况在沟通中我们往往不是专业翻译，因此在进行跨文化沟通的时候，需要尽量避免使用一些可能会造成误解或歧义的词语，尽可能做到言简意赅，不节外生枝。

not use the words that may cause ambiguity or misunderstanding. Instead, make sure that the wording is simple, straight and cut-to-the-point, so as not to cause unnecessary trouble.

In the beginning of cross-culture communication, be polite and use formal modes of address until it is made clear that you don't need to. Depending on the cultures that are interacting, this may include addressing others by first and last name, by last name alone, with a title such as "Mr.", or with one's office or position title such as commander Wang.

3. Avoid Non-verbal Offense

Non-verbal messages are no less important than verbal languages, and the forms of non-verbal message are varied, including body languages (such as eye contact, gestures, stance, etc.), paralanguage (such as speed, tone, volume) and dressing styles (for example, some clothes are only to be worn on certain occasions and circumstances).

In regarding to gestures, raising one's thumb in China means praise and complement, while in some other countries this gesture means severe insult. Similarly, pointing with an index finger, giving the "ok" sign, and other common gestures are alright in some cultures, while can be seen as offensive in some others. Since you may not know which gestures could be mistaken in this way, stick to "open handed" gestures. For instance, try using your whole hand if you need to point to something.

Know how to make or avoid eye contact is another important thing in cross cultural

应注意礼貌并使用正式称呼，直到被明确告知不必如此。不同文化中的正式称呼有所差异，例如称呼全名，仅称呼姓氏，称呼"先生"，或是加上某人的职务称呼，如"王班长"。

3. 避免非语言冒犯

在跨文化沟通中，非语言沟通同样重要。非语言的表达方式多样，包括肢体语言（如眼神、手势、站姿），副语言（如语速、语气、语调）和服饰（如特定身份或者特定时间、场合穿着的服饰）等。

在手势表达方面，竖大拇指在中国表示夸奖，然而某些国家却是表示侮辱的手势。同样，一些常用手势在不同文化中也有不同的意义。为避免误会，应多采用"张开双手"的手势，例如指示的时候用全手而非某个手指。

恰当的目光接触在跨文化沟通中非常重要。某些文

communication. In some cultures, looking another person in the eye when you speak is seen as a sign of honesty and interest. In other cultures, however, it may be seen as disrespectful or confrontational. Conversely, some cultures think that not looking a superior person in the eye when communicating is a sign of respect.

In terms of body distance, some cultures may require more personal space than others. If you are communicating with people from another culture and you find they get closer to you or farther away from you than you are used to, it's not necessarily the case that they are invading your space or trying to avoid you. Just try to follow their cues regarding personal space and communicate as best you can.

Above all, attention must be paid to the non-verbal details during cross-cultural communication, and it would be very helpful for both parties to learn about the cultural norms and customs of the opposite side beforehand, so as to avoid unintentional offenses.

11.3 Strategies of Cross-Cultural Communication

In an increasingly globalized market, managers often find themselves communicating with superiors and subordinates with different cultural backgrounds. Communicating across cultural divides poses special challenges for professionals, and the rise of Internet has further complicated the situation with its spontaneous respondence. Therefore, aside from the above skills

化中，保持对沟通对象的目光接触意味着尊重和感兴趣，而另外一些文化中则意味着不敬、挑衅，甚或在一些文化中，交谈中不直视上司是尊敬的表现。

不同文化对沟通时的身体距离有不同习惯。如果与来自其他文化的人交流时对方的沟通距离与自己的习惯不同，并非意味着对方试图进入你的私人空间或是要疏远你，尽量尝试彼此适应。

跨文化沟通中注意非语言的细节十分必要，双方在沟通前应尽量了解对方的文化习俗，以避免在沟通当中作出无意的冒犯。

三、跨文化管理策略

在全球化管理情境中，上下级往往来自不同的文化背景。特别是互联网的即时连接让跨文化沟通更加复杂。因此，在学习跨文化沟通技能的基础上，需要进一步了解跨文化管理策略。

and techniques, there are also broader strategies to follow in regard of cross-cultural communication.

1. Learning Different Cultures

In international business, managers should encourage cross-cultural communication, especially for multinational enterprises. Encourage them to get rid of cultural biases and learn from other cultures humbly.

Strengthen cross-cultural training. The contents of such training usually include: knowledge and understanding of other ethnic groups' culture and the culture of parent companies; cultural sensitivity and adaptability training; lectures on the languages, customs and life styles of exotic cultures; lectures on cross-cultural communication and the abilities to handle cross-cultural conflicts; lectures on the advanced management methods and operational concepts of foreign cultures, etc.

The overall objective is to enhance the employees' understanding and sensitivity toward foreign cultures through such training, to minimize cultural conflicts and to improve their abilities to handle cross-cultural conflicts during communication.

2. Building Up Cross-Cultural Communication Mechanism

A cross-cultural communication mechanism must be built up to facilitate communication among different cultural backgrounds through different kinds of organizations and

1. 学习异质文化

鼓励跨国企业管理者进行文化间交流，在新文化环境中摒弃偏见，虚心学习异质文化。

加强跨文化培训。培训内容一般包括：对他民族文化和母公司文化的认识和了解；文化的敏感性、适应性训练；语言、习俗、生活方式培训；跨文化沟通及冲突处理能力的培训；对先进的管理方法及经营理念的培训等。

通过跨文化学习，提高员工的文化认识和文化敏感性，引导员工理解和尊重对方的文化，减少文化冲突以及提高文化冲突的解决能力。

2. 建立跨文化沟通机制

不同文化背景的人彼此相处，应建立跨文化沟通的机制，通过各种正式的、有形的和无形的跨文化沟通组

communication channels, be them formal or informal, tangible or intangible.

The management of globalized enterprises need to adeptly adopt trans-national strategies to meet the common needs of human kind and the global market, in the meanwhile, strengthen the coordination and cooperation among headquarters and sub-branches, so as to establish a set of universal standards while acknowledging the diversified local cultures.

3. Implementing Localization Strategies

Localization strategy, especially personnel localization not only allow the company to make full use of local talents, improve business performances, reduce the cost of overseas dispatch and transnational operations, but it can also boost integration with local cultures and restrain the resistance of local society toward foreign capitals.

织与渠道。

跨国公司管理者应灵活运用跨国战略来满足人类普适性需求和全球市场，同时加强跨国企业总部和分部之间的协调合作，以建立起承认地方多样化的通用标准。

3. 实行本地化策略

实行本地化策略，特别是人员本地化，不但能充分利用当地人才为本公司服务，提高经营业绩以及降低跨国企业海外派遣人员和跨国经营的费用，而且还能更好地与当地文化融合，减少当地社会对外来资本的抵触情绪。

【Conclusion】本章小结

With the development of globalization, cross-cultural communication is getting more and more important for modern corporations, and it is of vital necessity to grasp a deepened understanding of cross-cultural communication. In this chapter, we discussed the dimensions of culture that can be influencers of cross-cultural communication. Skills and strategies of cross-cultural communication for corporations and businesses are discussed.

【Case Study】案例讨论

PLS is a multinational company headquartered in the United States. The company's vice president of human resources (Americans) talks to a Chinese employee who is considered to have potential for development. He wants to hear about his career development plan for the next five years and the position he hopes to achieve in the company. Instead of answering the questions positively, Chinese employees spent ten minutes talking about the future strategy of the company, its promotion system, and his current position in the company. The vice president gradually lost his patience to listen, because the same thing happened many times in his conversations with other Chinese employees. He began to look around, and even tried to interrupt the employee's conversation... After the conversation, the vice president complained to the HR manager of China, "I just want to know about the employee's development plan for the next five years, why can't he give me a definite answer?" The employees who attended the talks also complained to HR managers in China that "Vice President lacks patience to listen, even some aggressive, and seems to have no intention or interests of communicating with me". As a human resources manager in China, he understands that the communication between the two sides in different cultural backgrounds has created a gap between them.

Question:

Suppose you are the HR manager in China, how can you reduce the barriers to cross-cultural communication and improve the effectiveness of communication?

【Study Questions】课后问题

1. What are the dimensions of culture according to Hofstede?
2. What are the skills and techniques in cross-cultural communication?
3. Are there other strategies for cross-cultural communication that you would like to propose?

Section 3

Effective Communication Skills

第 3 篇 有效沟通技能

Chapter 12 Effective Speaking

第12章 有效演讲

In modern enterprise management, speaking is an essential skill. Through different types of presentations, individuals can transfer information to the audiences and achieve communication goals.

In this chapter, you will:
- know the elements of presentation;
- understand how to deliver an effective presentation;
- comprehend skills and techniques of presenting.

12.1 Definition and Types of Presentation

1. Elements of Presentation

Even in different situations, presentations have three common elements including the speaker, audience and information which constitute the most basic structure of communication.

(1) The speaker.

The speaker, who is responsible for the presentation or performance, is the starting point of one-way communication and the sender of information. The speaker can convey necessary information by oral language, visual slides or other means to achieve his/her own purpose. The presentation content, verbal expression, body

现代企业管理中,演讲是必不可少的技能。通过不同类型的演讲,能够进行信息传递,以达到沟通目的。

本章将阐述演讲元素;有效的演讲结构的构建方法以及演讲技巧。

一、演讲的定义与类型

1. 演讲的要素

演讲具有三要素——演讲者、观众和信息,三者构成了信息沟通最基本的结构。

(1)演讲者。

演讲者,即在演讲中主要负责进行展示或表演的人,是单向信息沟通的出发点、信息的输出者。演讲者能够以口头语言、媒体展示等方式传递信息,以达到自己的目的。成功的演讲者不仅是

language, facial expressions, coping ability and so on of the speaker will have a crucial impact on the output of the presentation. We can say that the speaker is the key to a presentation. A good speaker should be not only an excellent expresser and performer, but also a good listener who can pay attention to the reactions, expressions and attitudes of the audience and give appropriate feedback.

(2) Audience.

The audience is the receiver of information in one-way communication. After receiving the information conveyed by the speaker, the audience makes their own understanding and forms feedback based on self-cognition. The same information or opinion is received differently by different audiences. The audience is usually related to the scene. For example, in the internal meeting of the enterprise, the audiences are mostly colleagues or superiors. In this kind of presentation, the speaker needs to clarify his/her department's position and express the core opinions for subsequent discussion. While audiences at large associational conferences are mostly mixed, with different identities, occupations, and backgrounds. This kind of presentation requires the speaker to consider the characteristics of different audiences and choose the most effective and appropriate way to convey information.

(3) Information.

Information, which is the content that the speaker attempts to convey and the audience

一个优秀的表演者，也是一个优秀的倾听者，从听众反应、表情、态度等方面收集反馈信息。

（2）观众。

观众是单向沟通的信息接收方。观众在接收了演讲者传递出的信息后在自我认知的基础上作出自己的理解并形成反馈。不同场景下的听众特征存在差异。例如企业会议听众和协会会议听众的身份背景，以及聆听演讲的目的存在不同，需要演讲者仔细辨析，选择合适的方式传递信息。

（3）信息。

信息，即演讲者企图传递、观众最终接收的内容，

eventually receive, is the part shared by the speaker and the audience in one-way information communication. The presentation process is equivalent to a communication process, which inevitably leads to the deviation of information transmission. The information that the speaker intends to convey is influenced by the audience's own position, education, background and other factors, resulting in different understandings, which may be different from the speaker's original intention.

2. The Communication Process of Presentation

In many cases, presentation is regarded as a one-way communication, where information is transmitted unilaterally by the speaker to the audience and then understood and absorbed by the audience. In fact, an effective presentation is a two-way communication process (See Figure 12.1).

是单向信息沟通中由演讲者与观众共享的部分。需要注意的是演讲者企图传递的信息受到观众自身的立场、教育水平、生活背景等因素影响从而产生了不同的理解，很可能与演讲者的本意有所差异。

2. 演讲沟通过程

在很多情况下，人们认为演讲是一个从演讲者到听众的单向沟通过程，然而事实上真正有效的演讲是一个双向沟通的过程。

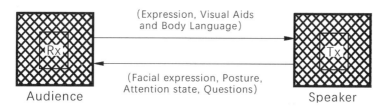

Figure 12.1　The Two-way Communication Process
图 12.1　双向沟通过程

From the approach of two-way communication process, the speaker conveys information by his/her own expression, visual aids and body language, and then receives feedbacks from the audience

演讲者通过自己的语言表达、媒体材料、肢体语言等方式传递信息，而后得到观众的反馈，进而对于可能

through facial expressions, posture, attention state, questions, etc. Based on the feedbacks, the speaker could evaluate how his or her viewpoint is accepted by the audience and could give further explanation on the misunderstood part. This can help the speaker reduce the information distortion in the process of communication and finally achieve his/her desired communication goals. This process is not just one time but repeated throughout the whole presentation process, from beginning to the end. Good speakers can constantly adjust their presentation methods and encourage the audience to actively ask questions as a way of giving feedbacks.

3. Types of Presentation

According to the different types of interaction, it can be divided into one-way presentation, interactive presentation and guiding presentation.

One-way presentation refers to the presentation that the speaker mainly outputs information to the audience.

Interactive presentation refers to the presentation where information is mainly delivered by the speaker but feedbacks and further information communication also take place between the speaker and the audience. It is the mainstream presentation type at present.

Guiding presentation refers to the presentation in which the audience has been given certain information or materials in advance

误解或一知半解的信息作出解释，减少信息失真，最终达到预期效果。

优秀的演讲者在整个演讲过程中都会鼓励听众反馈，通过收集反馈信息适当调整演讲方式。

3. 演讲类型

根据与观众的互动方式不同可划分三种演讲类型。

单向式演讲主要由演讲者向观众进行单向信息输出，多为信息发布或事件通知。

互动式演讲指在主要由演讲者传递信息但能够在演讲者与观众之间形成反馈与进一步信息沟通的演讲，是目前主流的演讲方式。

引导式演讲指事先提供给观众一定信息或材料，由演讲者鼓励观众提问、发表

and the speaker encourages the audience to ask questions and make comments during the presentation. Compared with the first two kinds of presentation types, it is more interactive and challenging. It is more common in the lessons and trainings.

12.2 Structure of Presentation

In order to improve the effectiveness of a speech, the speaker needs to have a well-designed presentation structure, which generally includes four parts: opening, main content, conclusion and Q&A (questions and answers).

1. Opening

There is a saying, "A good beginning is half done." It is truly so for a presentation. Opening refers to the introduction part before entering the main content, which usually includes greetings, small talk, self-introduction, topic introduction, scene construction etc. Different openings can be designed according to the content of the speech, but they should generally meet the following requirements.

First, the opening should show the credibility of the speaker. Credibility is largely determined by the speaker's professionalism, title and status, background, and the purpose of the presentation. Experts who are widely recognized in a certain professional field naturally have higher credibility. However, building credibility in a short time

评论，相对于前两种演讲方式互动性更强，更具有挑战性，常见于教学培训中。

二、演讲的结构

为了增强演讲效果，需要设计一个好的演讲结构，一般包括四个部分，分别为开场白、主体内容，结尾和问答。

1. 开场白

开场白指的是演讲者在正式进入演讲内容前的引入部分，通常包括自我介绍、话题引入、场景构建等环节。根据演讲内容可以设计不同的开场白，但一般应满足以下要求。

开场白的可信度很大程度上取决于演讲者的专业性、资历背景、过去的成就以及所表现出的演讲目的。读者可以参考本书第2章关于增加沟通者可信度的内容，思考如何增加演讲者的可信度。

for an unknown speaker is a real challenge. The most basic method is through introduction by the host or by the speaker himself. A convincing background introduction is helpful to improve the trust from the audiences. Excessive boasting should be avoided, which tends to be distasteful. Specifically, you can refer to the tips mentioned in Chapter 2 to increase the credibility of speakers.

Secondly, in the opening of the presentation, the speaker should arouse the audience's interest. The speaker needs to establish a good relationship with the audience, for example, by designing some stories or performances, so that emotional resonance is more easily to take place. The speaker can also use some skills, such as activating the atmosphere with jokes, or raising some questions to create suspense, etc. Remember that the opening should not be too long. For a twenty minutes' presentation, usually 2～3 minutes for opening is recommended. A long opening may distract audience's concentration, causing the difficulty to accepting main content.

Finally, the opening should bring in the topic of the presentation, to pave the way for the discussion to be launched in the main part, so as to stimulate the desire and curiosity of the audience.

Check the following questions when preparing the opening part.

(1) Who are you to them?

(2) Where do you speak?

(3) Who are the audience?

(4) What style of presentation do you want to give?

演讲者通过开场白激发听众兴趣。可以通过小故事、笑话，或是提问吸引听众兴趣。开场白不宜过长，对于20分钟的演讲，开场白通常以2～3分钟为宜。

开场白应带入演讲主题，为在主体部分将要展开的论述进行铺垫。从而激发听众的欲望与好奇。

可以通过回答以下问题检验开场白准备得充分与否。

(5) What is the audience's focus?

(6) What's your theme?

2. Main Content (Body)

The main content is an essential part to an entire presentation. The speaker needs to design the theme based on the purpose of the presentation, which usually includes one main theme and several subthemes, and then establish the whole structure and put forward arguments.

The structure of argument is the skeleton of the whole presentation, which generally includes vertical structure, horizontal structure and combined structure. Vertical structure refers to the argumentation structure formed according to the vertical order including development process and time axis. The basic logic is "narrative-analysis-conclusion". The application needs to emphasize the key points and draw conclusions. Horizontal structure refers to the argumentation structure formed from the parallel angles including components, attributes and observation modes of things. The basic logic is "analysis-summing-analysis-summing-conclusions". The horizontal structure is suitable to interpret comprehensive themes. Combined structure is the combination of the two structures, which is more complex and challenging for the speaker.

An argument is a set of points in a presentation. Select main points based on the length of your presentation. The speaker should decide what statements, facts, and points best illustrate the theme of your presentation. According to

2. 主体内容

演讲的主体部分是整个演讲的核心，演讲者需要针对演讲的大主题与分主题建立表达结构并形成论点。

表达结构相当于整个演讲的骨架。表达结构通常包括纵向结构、横向结构以及两者结合的纵横结构。纵向结构指按照事物发展过程、时间轴等纵向顺序形成的论证结构，通常为"叙述—分析—结论"。横向结构是指按照事物的组成部分、属性、观察方式等平行角度形成的论证结构，通常为"分析—总结—分析—总结—结论"。纵横结构是将两种结构结合，在一类结构的基础上加入另一类结构，属于较为复杂的逻辑结构。

论点是演讲中的一系列观点。演讲的论点不宜过多，应选取对主题最具支撑力的观点作为论点。根据听众记忆曲线，演讲的主体部分也

Audience's Memory Curve, the main content of the speech is also the stage where the audience's attention is easily distracted. The refining of viewpoints can help the audience understand the speech better, which should be simple and clear, normally limited to 2～5 points.

For example, a 10～20 minutes' presentation, should include no more than 3 points. Just like TED talks which are popular all over the world. The average time length of a TED talk is 18 minutes, and the theme is supported by three points. The speaker should also consider the way the points relate to one another, and be prepared to discuss them in a logical, cohesive fashion.

3. Ending

A good ending emphasizes on the theme of the presentation, and will leave the audience with a deep impression. Some obvious transitional words should be used at the end to indicate that it is time to move on to the end. At the ending, the speaker can achieve his goal by:

(1) concluding the previous presentation;
(2) giving answer to the questions put forward at the opening;
(3) calling for actions.

12.3 Skills and Techniques

The on-site performance will ultimately determine the effectiveness of communication. The speaking techniques include psychological adjustment before presentation, verbal

是听众注意力容易分散的阶段，通过观点的提炼可以帮助听众更好地理解演讲内容。同时，观点应该简要明了，一般归纳为2～5个。

举例来说，10～20分钟的演讲不应超过三个论点。正如风靡世界的TED演讲一样，TED演讲的标准时长大约18分钟，一个主题下基本由3个观点构成支撑。演讲者需要设计观点之间的逻辑关系。

3. 结尾

在结尾部分应对全文观点进行总结强调，给听众留下深刻印象。

可使用一些明显的过渡提示进入结尾部分：总结、解答或呼吁感召。

三、演讲技巧

演讲技巧包括演讲前的心理调整、演讲中的语言沟通与非语言沟通，以及辅助媒体材料的准备与使用配合。

communication and nonverbal communication in presentation, and the preparation and use of auxiliary media materials.

1. Psychological Adjustment

For most people, speaking in front of a large crowd is quite stressful. Usually the speaker sees this tension as fear, which may seriously defeat confidence. In fact, a moderate degree of tension is helpful for the speaker to focus and to achieve a certain state of mental excitement.

For speakers prone to excessive tension, the following psychological adjustment techniques may help:
- Get familiar with the site in advance;
- Rehearse and make some adjustment;
- Take a deep breath;
- Give yourself psychological hint and tell yourself that everything is ready and just be relax.

The key of psychological adjustment before a presentation is to create a moderate sense of tension. This varies from person to person, and has something to do with the speaker's personality, habits and so on. Every speaker needs to find techniques to calm down before giving a presentation.

The speaker should show confidence. Before the presentation, the speaker should be confident that the communication goal could be achieved through engaging in this presenting process. If the

1. 心理调整

公众演讲对于大多数人而言是一种压力,特别是紧张感被视作惧怕,或将打击演讲者的自信。事实上,适度的紧张感有利于帮助演讲者集中注意力,达到一定的精神兴奋状态。

对于易过度紧张的演讲者,心理调整的技巧包括在演讲前有规律地深呼吸;提前进入会场熟悉环境,适度走动;进行一定心理暗示,放松自己的心情;事先进行彩排并对已有内容进行调整修改;运用眼神接触等。

演讲前的心理调整目的是创造适度紧张感。这种紧张感因人而异。

演讲者应表现出自信。在演讲之前,演讲者应该确信,投入的演讲就可以达到沟通目标,否则听众对演讲

speaker is unsure of this, the audiences will be less convinced to the message.

2. Verbal Communication

Presentation is the art of language communication. Language is the carrier of information. Effective verbal communication is necessary in business. You need good communication to do everything from performing your job properly to negotiate with your supplier. The speaker should pay attention to the accuracy, understandability, personalization and visualization of language expression.

Firstly, the language in a presentation must be accurate, concise and clear. Audiences will lose interest to a speech that is composed of vague vocabulary. Irrelevant elements should be limited or removed in the speech. Focus on the theme and strengthen the statements so that audiences can respond accordingly. Verbal communication is different than other forms of communication in that it is easier to get off topic, which can make it hard to remember what the conversation was really supposed to be about.

Secondly, always include a consideration for your audience when planning out a speech. You don't want to say something that might be taken the wrong way or offend your audience. Be careful of using sarcasm in a speech. From the standpoint of an audience, a sarcastic remark requires a process of decoding and interpretation before they can understand what has been said, what has been meant.

内容就很难信服。

2. 语言沟通

演讲是一门语言沟通艺术，语言是信息的载体，是完成企业管理和商业活动的重要因素。演讲者需要注意语言表达的准确性、易懂性、个性化与形象化。

演讲的语言应准确简明，生涩的词句会让听众失去兴趣。演讲中应减少不相关要素，聚焦于主题和论点以便于听众记忆和理解。

沟通中应考虑听众的感受。演讲者不希望被听众误解或是感到冒犯。在演讲中使用讽刺应谨慎，因为听众可能无法理解。

Thirdly, try to incorporate humor. Everyone likes to laugh, so humor can be a great way to lighten up your speech and make your audiences more receptive to your message. Of course, you should avoid vulgar or inappropriate humor to avoid offending your audiences.

3. Nonverbal Communication

Nonverbal communication, which includes paralanguage (vocal) and body language, plays an essential role in presentation. Many people pay great attention to the acceptance and correctness of the verbal communication and overlook the influence and cultural difference of nonverbal communication. So, in the process of delivering a presentation, it is not complete while ignoring nonverbal communication. Nonverbal communication mainly includes paralanguage, body language and visual aids.

使用幽默。适度幽默可以让演讲充满活力并帮助听众理解，但应避免粗俗和不合时宜的幽默以免冒犯听众。

3. 非语言沟通

非语言沟通主要包括副语言和肢体语言，在演讲中扮演重要角色。很多人对语言沟通中的词句非常重视而忽视了非语言沟通的影响和文化差异。在演讲中，忽视非语言沟通是不完整的。

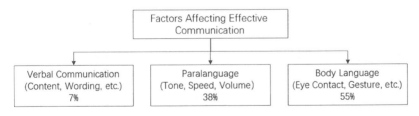

Figure 12.2　Factors Affecting Effective Communication
图 12.2　沟通的影响要素

(1) Paralanguage.
① Speed.
Speed is how fast or slow the speaker speaks. If the speaker speaks too fast, the audience may not hear clearly. If the speaker speaks too slowly, the audience may become distracted and unable to

（1）副语言。
①语速。
语速是说话的速度。语速过快会导致听众听不清楚，语速过慢会导致听众注意力分散。演讲者可以通过调整

effectively receive information. The speaker can guide the audience's attention to the key points of the presentation by adjusting the speed of expression.

② Volume.

Volume is the intensity of the sound. In presentation, the volume is related to the situation of the venue, sound equipment, speaker's content control and other factors. Try to make sure that the audience who is furthest away can hear clearly and the audience who is nearest can also accept the volume instead of being too harsh.

③ Tone.

Tone is the pronunciation changes of high and low. Speakers can express different emotions through different tones and adjust based on different reactions of the audience, such as the rising tone to express surprise and appeal. The use of tone is a hard subject that requires a speaker to learn through practice.

④ Pause.

Pause is deliberate silence in the process of presentation. Pause can leave the audiences some time to make a deep thinking. The speaker could also use pause to arouse the audience's interest and generate curiosity about the following content.

(2) Body language.

① Eye contact.

Making and maintaining eye contact is crucial when speaking to people, whether one-on-one or in a group setting. It shows attentiveness and interest in what's being said. Increased eye contact is associated with credibility and

语速以引导听众关注重要内容。

② 音量。

音量指演讲声音的大小，演讲者的音量应随着场地大小、设备、内容控制等而变化，使场地中每一位听众可以舒适地听清说话内容。

③ 语调。

语调是发音高低的变化。演讲者可以通过语调表达不同情绪，例如用升调表达惊喜和吸引力。语调的使用需要演讲者通过经验来学习。

④ 停顿。

停顿会让观众有时间进行深入思考。演讲者还可以利用暂停来激发听众的兴趣，使其对后续内容产生好奇。

（2）身体语言。

① 目光接触。

沟通中保持目光接触至关重要。目光接触传递了关注和兴趣，可以增加可信度。但是，演讲者应该力争与会场中每一位听众进行目光接

dominance, so it is important to maintain solid eye contact when making a presentation. The speaker should try to make eye contact with each audience in the venue instead of looking at one audience for more than 5 seconds which is too personal for a group of audiences.

② Smile.

This is especially important when presenting to groups of people because it is a simple way to build a foundational relationship with people you may not have any one-on-one interaction with. Smiling helps us form and sustain interpersonal relationships, so it is an essential part of body language in presentation.

③ Posture.

Standing posture reflects the speaker's temperament. A natural posture can help establish a confident and professional image. During the presentation, the speaker should pay attention that: Do not sway at random; Do not be too casual, such as leaning on the platform; Face the audience; Do not be too stiff.

④ Body movement.

The body movement reflects the status of the speaker. The speaker's movements should be natural, not static or deliberate. In presentation, the speaker can: Design moving lines according to venue. Move with purpose. For example, to show the important content on the slide, the speaker can move near to the screen and directly points at that content and interact with the audience. Avoid random, repetitive and frequent moving. A too complex moving line may distract the audience.

触而不应长时间与某一位听众进行目光接触，过度关注某个人会让其他听众感到不适。

② 微笑。

在演讲中保持微笑非常重要，微笑有助于我们形成和维持人际关系，因此它是沟通中重要的身体语言。

③ 姿势。

站姿反映了演讲者的气质。自然的姿势有助于树立自信和专业的形象。演讲者应注意避免不得体的姿势。

④ 身体移动。

身体移动反映了演讲者的状态。演讲者的动作应该是自然的，而不应过于静止或过度刻意。演讲者可以根据现场情况设计移动线路；结合演讲有目的地移动和动作；避免随意、重复和频繁移动。过于复杂的移动路线可能会分散观众的注意力。

⑤ Gesture.

Gesture mainly refers to the hand action taken in the presentation by the speaker. The speakers can pay attention to the following points: Combine gestures with their daily habits to find their own characteristics. Not to be too strong and should be matched to their style of presentation. Not to be too much or too repetitive in case of affecting the audience's concentration.

(3) Visual aids.

In actual presentation, visual aids, such as slides, can make use of the audience's vision to give them space to think on the basis of auditory information and enhance their understanding. Combining words and images is more conducive to the audience's memory than simple images. Visual aids can help increase the variety, interest and richness of the presentation. Through visual aids, the presentation can make more changes and achieve more effective results.

⑤手势。

手势动作，主要指演讲者在演讲过程中采取的手部动作。演讲者在演讲中的手势动作应结合自己的日常习惯与演讲风格，发现自己的特色。

（3）视觉辅助工具。

幻灯片等视觉辅助工具能够利用观众的视觉在听觉获取的信息基础上给予观众思考的空间，增强观众的理解。文字与图像的结合能够增加演讲整体的变化性、趣味性与丰富性，更利于观众记忆。

【Conclusion】本章小结

Presentation includes three common elements: the speaker, audience and information, which also constitute the most basic structure of communication. The speaker, who is responsible for the presentation or performance, is the starting point of one-way communication and the sender of information. The audience, who is the individual or organization watching the presentation, is the end point and receiver of one-way communication. Information, which is the content that the speaker attempts to convey and the audience eventually receive.

A presentation structure mainly includes four parts: opening, main content, conclusion and question and answer (Q&A). According to the different types of interaction, it can be divided into one-way presentation, interactive presentation and guiding presentation. According to the presentation purpose, presentation can be divided into tell presentation, sell presentation, entertainment presentation, debate presentation.

Generally speaking, techniques include psychological adjustment before presentation, verbal communication and nonverbal communication in presentation, and the preparation and use of visual aids. A moderate degree of tension is helpful for the speaker to focus and to achieve a certain state of mental excitement. The speaker should pay attention to the accuracy, understandability, personalization and visualization of language expression.

【Exercises】实务练习

How to Make Effective PowerPoint Slides?

An overall concept is necessary to design a slide. A good framework and basic design can greatly reduce the difficulty of subsequent design.

(1) Opening & Ending: Most slides need opening and ending slide. The content can be varied under different occasions, for example adding main theme of introductive story in the opening slide, inviting questions from the audience at the ending page.

(2) Transfer presentation frame to slides: Framework of slide can be established on the basis of content framework. The core is agenda slides at the beginning and closing slides at the end. Those two parts respectively emphasize the information the audience should receive. In the design of these two categories of slide, you should remember to use headline to ensure the eye-catching effect.

(3) Re-use agenda slides: Insert the agenda slides at the end of each part to highlight what the next section will tell. The application of agenda slides have the effect of the directory, reminding the audience the content of previous parts.

(4) Make full use of the slide master: A simple and beautiful slide master can help ensure some necessary general information and promise convenience in the later design.

(5) Pay attention to the combination of color and font settings: The combination

of the slide color will give the audience the most intuitionistic first impression. The overall color selection should not be too complex. The color collocation should be the one that is more easy to see which is usually a dark background with a light font or a light background with a dark font. To the parts needed to be emphasized, a few bold color can be chosen. However, remember to use properly. Do not choose fonts that are too fancy and difficult to understand. Font size selection should take factors like content distribution and site conditions etc., into account.

Single slide design usually refers to the design of backup slides that are not opening slide, ending slide, agenda slides and closing slides. Backup slides are slides whose function is to support points raised in agenda slides.

(1) Information Headline: Information headline is the summary of single slide but need to make difference with the main theme. The headline should be a phrase or short sentence that simply and clearly convey the message to the audience, such as the Forbes Business Ranking. Headlines need to be enlarged or highlighted with bold colors for emphasis.

(2) Chart and Graph: Chart refers to the image expression based on data, while graph refers to the relationship structure and logical thinking of the construction of various concepts. The use of charts and graphs can intuitively show the changes and comparisons of data and directly show the relationship between various concepts. The efficiency of information should be paid attention to in the design of charts and graphs. The chart and graph should only use and display relevant data and delete unnecessary diagrams to ensure that the overall image is easy to understand.

(3) Concise Content: Backup slides should not include too much content. Slides are a presentation aid, not a screen that completely shows the content of a speaker's presentation. Slides need to attract the attention of the audience. If the slide is full of information, the audience will lose interest in the speaker's presentation and the whole presentation tend to be too jumbled and difficult to view.

Please try to make PowerPoint slides on the topic of "How to make effective speaking".

 【Study Questions】课后问题

1. What are the elements of presentation structure?
2. What are the requirements of verbal communication in presentation?
3. What can the speaker do to adjust his psychological state before the presentation?
4. Try to form a presentation structure based on a recent business news that you are interested.

Chapter 13　Resume and Job Application Letter

第13章　撰写简历

A resume is the basis for finding a suitable job for yourself. Before you are ready to enter the workplace or transfer to a new one, you need to carefully evaluate yourself and plan your career development to complete a resume that maximizes your value. A good resume can't just be a list of past experiences. It needs to analyze the purpose of job hunting and employer's needs, process existing information, choose the right media and organize content.

By the end of this chapter, you will be able to:
- understand the definition, purpose and type of resume;
- master the skills to write resumes and job application letters.

简历是求职的基础，简历应在自我评估和职业发展规划基础上，最大化体现自身价值和特色。一份好的简历不能仅罗列过往经历，还需要分析求职目的和雇主需求、对信息加工处理、选择正确的媒介并组织内容。

通过本章的学习，你将能够了解简历的定义、用途和类型；掌握撰写简历和求职信的技能。

13.1　The Basics of Resume

一、求职简历基础

1. What Is a Resume?

1. 简历的定义

A resume is a highly personalized and persuasive summary of a person's background, experience, education, and skill level that shows your qualifications for a job with a specific employer.

A well-written resume will have a profound

简历是对一个人背景、经历、教育程度和技能水平的高度个性化和有说服力的总结，其显示了为特定雇主工作的资格。

良好的简历会对整个职

influence throughout your career. Resume may leave an important first impression on your potential employer. It opens a window for an employer to know about you. When you are employed, keeping your resume up-to-date may help you take advantage of all possible chances for a better development. It will help you form a clear picture of who you are right now and show your potential for suitable job vacant.

2. Types of Resume

According to format, resume can be mainly divided into chronological resume, functional resume and combination resume (See Table 13.1).
(1) Chronological resume.

A chronological resume is a resume format that displays work experience in chronological order. It is more suitable for job seekers with rich relevant experience or inexperienced freshmen than other forms of resume. For the former, job seekers can emphasize their professionalism and accumulated resources in relevant fields by presenting their own experiences. For the latter, the freshmen have insufficient work experience, thus the display of work experience can emphasize their adaptability and show themselves from different angles.

The chronological resume requires the job seeker to write his/her work experience of the job seeker in reverse order, including time, job description and responsibilities, work performance and achievement. The most important tips of writing a chronological resume is to highlight the key points and adjust the expression and display mode around

业生涯产生深远的影响。求职中，简历可能会给潜在雇主留下重要的第一印象。在求职过程中，保持简历的最新状态可能有助于你利用一切可能的机会获得更好的发展。

2. 简历的类型

简历主要分为按时间顺序的简历、功能性简历和组合式简历。
（1）时序型简历。

时序型简历是指按照时间顺序对工作经历进行罗列展示的简历格式，适合拥有丰富经验的从业者以及缺乏经验的应届生。有经验的求职者可以强调专业性和在相关领域积累的资源；新手求职者工作经验的展示可以强调其适应性，以从不同角度展现自己。

时序型简历的书写需要将求职者的工作经历按照时间倒叙书写，内容包括工作时间，工作内容与职责，工作表现与业绩等。要领是根据主要工作经验突出关键词，优化表达和格式。

its own advantages or key work experiences.

In terms of advantages, it is more convenient for job seekers to write a chronological resume. Based on previous self-evaluation, the initial resume framework which can reflect the job habits and preferences of job seekers in different work environments can be completed. The job seekers with rich experience will have the chance to demonstrate their qualifications to the greatest extent possible. In terms of weakness, chronological resume can easily become a simple work experience list, lacking the sparkle to attract recruiters.

(2) Functional resume.

A functional resume is a resume that emphasizes the skills, abilities, qualifications, achievements, etc. of a job seeker but not related to a particular employer. Compared with the structure of "doing something at some time in a certain company" in chronological resume, the functional resume emphasizes the content of "doing something and get some result". This type of resume is suitable for job seekers whose working experiences are relatively limited, or who want to change industry or profession.

The functional resume requires the applicant to display the characteristics and advantages through structured content including the skills, job achievements and work abilities. Functional resume writing needs to emphasis on one's own advantages to match the position in previous work experiences and strengthen the capability of the applicant.

In terms of advantages, the functional resume can show the ability and achievements of the

时序型简历的优点在于求职者撰写较为方便，基于自我评价梳理即可完成初步简历框架，能够反映求职者的工作习惯与偏好，经验丰富的从业者可最大程度展示其资历。在缺点方面，时序型简历很容易变为简单的工作经历罗列，缺少吸引招聘者的闪光点。

（2）功能型简历。

功能型简历强调求职者的技能、能力、资历、资质、成就等内容但不与特定的雇主相联系。相对于时序型简历"在某时某地做某事"，功能型简历强调"做某事得到某结果"。这类简历适合有相对有限的工作经历的求职者，或是想要更换行业或职业的求职者。

求职者通过结构性文字内容展示求职者的特点与优势，包括技能、工作成就与工作能力。需要求职者提炼出自身与职位相匹配的优势，通过展示相关能力与经验加强说服力。

功能型简历能够最大程度展示求职者的能力和成就，

job seeker to the greatest extent and focus on the target job requirements. For job seekers who have a large gap between jobs, a functional resume can make up this problem. However, it takes more time to write than a chronological resume. Also, redundant information will confuse the recruiters, and fail to get a good first impression.

(3) Combination resume.

The combination resume is a resume that combines a chronological resume with a functional resume. It enhances the format of a chronological resume, but the contents highlight the relevant skills, abilities and advantages for the target position like functional resume. This type of resume avoids the use of a text-based resume format, which is more clear and specific.

并聚焦招聘需求。求职者可用功能型简历一定程度上掩盖工作间差距较大的问题。然而其撰写更耗时，信息冗杂可能会带来不好的第一印象。

（3）复合型简历。

复合型简历将时序型简历与功能型简历相结合，强化时序型简历的格式，但内容上针对目标岗位突出了相关的技能、能力与优势。其避免了基于文本的简历格式，更清晰具体。

Table 13.1　The Types of Resume According to Format
表 13.1　简历类型对比

Types	Characteristics	Strength	Weakness
Chronological Resume	Display work experience in chronological order.	More convenient to write; Favorable for the job seekers with rich experience to demonstrate their qualifications.	May easily become a simple work experience list; May lack the sparkle to attract recruiters.
Functional Resume	Emphasize the skills, abilities, qualifications, achievements, etc.	Show the ability and achievements to the greatest extent; Mask the large gap between jobs.	Takes more time; May lead to redundant information, causing confusion.
Combination Resume	Combine a chronological resume with a functional resume.	Avoid to raise the doubt or rejection of the recruiter; Be more specific to a target position for applicants.	Takes more time; May cause chaos in the whole resume format.

In addition to the above main types of resumes, resumes also have record-based resumes, target-based resumes and resource-based resumes.

Record-based resume is the resume that only need to list technically relevant materials, suitable for professional and technical personnel. For example, in doctors' resume, putting the information of education, qualifications, internships, in-service hospitals and published papers in a record-based format is quite persuasive.

A target-based resume is a resume in which job seekers clearly emphasizes the skills and abilities that fitting in well with the target job.

A resource-based resume is a resume suits those job seekers who do not know what career they want to pursue, thus emphasizing achievements and skills in a broader way.

在上述主要简历类型之外，简历亦有履历型简历、目标型简历和资源型简历。

履历型简历只需罗列技术相关材料，适合专业技术人员，如医生。

目标型简历，求职者对于职位了解极为透彻，明确强调其适合目标工作的技能。

资源型简历，求职者不清楚自己要从事什么职业，比较宽泛地强调成就和技能。

13.2　Preparation for a Resume

1. Self- Evaluation

Self-evaluation is the first step of developing a good resume. Before you start writing a resume, you need to first think about your strengths and weaknesses, interest, skills, etc.

二、求职简历的前期准备

1. 自我评估

书写简历前，求职者需要首先进行自我评估，如技能、行业、工作风格、工作期望等。

You may refer to the following questions:
(1) What skills do you have?
(2) What is your strength and weakness?
(3) What industry do you want to work in? Your present industry or another new industry?
(4) What kind of working style do you prefer? Would you prefer firm deadlines

or flexible schedule? Would you prefer specific instructions or freedom and uncertainty? Would you prefer independent work or team work? Do you like challenge? Are you comfortable with pressure?

(5) What kind of achievement do you want to make?

(6) Where do you want to work? In company or at home? How will you react to frequent business travel?

(7) How fast do you want to move up? Which position do you finally want to be promoted to?

(8) Is there any policies or requirements that you want to insist? Do you want to achieve certain purposes or values? Is the culture and ethical standard important for you?

(9) What is your requirement for salary, bonus and vacation?

Through self-evaluation, you will be more aware of the current situation and future career development. Well-organized information laid the foundation for resume writing. A clear understanding of the target position can also help you become more effective in job search.

2. Building Personal Branding

Personal branding is a popular term of marketing yourself. It not only involves the skills and work experience that is included in the resume, but also shows overall image, such as personality, social circle, resources, etc. A more comprehensive personality can be shown to the recruiters.

Nowadays, personal branding can be enhanced through a variety of social network circle, such as WeChat, LinkedIn, Blogs, Facebook. Your experience, knowledge, value and vision increase the chances for job hunting

通过自我评估，求职者能够整体把握目前自身的情况与未来的职业发展方向，为简历撰写做好准备，让求职更富效率。

2. 塑造个人品牌形象

塑造个人品牌形象不仅包括简历中所体现的技能与工作经验等，也展示自己的整体风貌，如性格、社交圈、资源等，可以向招募者展示全面的形象。

个人品牌可以通过各种社交网络圈实现。经验、知识、价值等通过在线社交媒体传播从而增加了就业机会。

through online social media.

3. Job Seek Channels

After completing the resume and personal branding, job seekers need to find their own target work through various channels. Channels could be online job searching platforms, social networking, internship, etc.

Once taken some time to polish the resume, the job seeker may try searching for openings online, browsing various job search sites. Many companies will allow prospective employees to apply for a position online.

The university students may also go through the job board hosted by university. Attending job fairs, working with a recruiting service, and networking with other professionals can also better their chances of entering a new field.

Many experts consider networking as the most important channel especially for career advancement. Networking can start with familiar people including friends, family members, classmates, teammates, and colleagues. The job seekers can join the alumni association to find alumni in business which he/she targets. They can also make full use of the social media talked above. With the personal branding, they may expand their professional social circle.

Internship is also a useful tool for job hunting, especially for those graduates. Many companies use intern program to find full-time employees. For those interns, even if the intern doesn't lead to a full-time job, it will provide them

3. 求职渠道

职位发布渠道包括网络求职平台；社交网络；实习等。

润色简历后，求职者可在线寻找空缺职位。许多公司允许在线申请职位。

大学的就业办公室、招聘会、招聘服务机构以及与专业人士建立的联系，均是很有帮助的求职渠道。

许多专家认为网络是重要职业发展渠道。网络可以从熟悉的人开始，包括朋友、家人、同学、队友和同事。求职者可以加入校友协会，还可以充分利用社交媒体。

实习也是有效的求职工具，尤其对于毕业生而言。许多公司使用实习生计划来寻找全职员工。对于实习生来说，实习是了解这个职业

with a chance for insight into the profession.

13.3 Write A Resume

The information in a resume includes name and contact information, capabilities and skills, education, achievement, working experience, and activities.

1. Name and Contact Information

Write full name of the applicant on the head of the resume. Choose an appropriate font size. The contact information should include telephone number, phone number, email address, and sometimes mailing address. Make sure the email address is professional and avoid using nicknames or being childish, sexy, illicit or inappropriate personal email address. Remember to remove the hyperlinks in the resume. If you have a networking website, you can also list it.

2. Capabilities and Skills

In this section, the applicants need to show their qualification of skills and capabilities by summarizing, instead of just listing, the knowledge and achievements of specific field. Nontechnical skills are better to be proofed with figures or other persuasive materials.

3. Education

In Education part, the information on education background is essential including the name of institution, major, degree, courses that is related to career, etc. You can also list your GPA

的良好机会。

三、简历撰写

简历信息包括姓名与联系方式、能力、教育、成就、工作经历以及其他信息。

1. 姓名和联系方式

简历上方书写求职者的名字，使用合适的字号。联系方式需要包括电话、手机、邮箱或住址。邮箱需要保证专业性，避免不妥当的邮箱名称。简历中应去掉超链接。

2. 技能

在技能部分，申请人需要展示其技能和能力的资格。求职者需要总结其专业知识和所获成就，在列举时需要用数据等可信资料突出亮点。

3. 教育背景

在教育背景部分，学历信息需要包括学院、专业、学位以及相关课程。若绩点高于3.0也可以列出。学位按

A Sample Resume

Minghui Wang

(86)21-13764362385   minghui.wang@ecnu.edu.cn

Education

East China Normal University   Graduation Date: June 2019
Bachelor of Business Science   GPA:3.7
Major: Business Analyzing   Minor: Finance

Work Experience

Intern

Shanghai Bank

- Managed cash forecast report and gross profit margin report
- Utilized Microsoft Excel for daily tasks in spreadsheets and formulas
- Gain insight into process to develop an understanding of the front line of banking

Activities

President of Student Union

- Put forward several proposals based on students' interests
- Formed the student independent management team and the management plan
- Host the monthly meeting of all student union members and make decisions based on common sense

Skills & Capabilities

Database Software: Microsoft Access, Microsoft SQL Server
Operating Syatem: Microsoft Windows 10, Linus, Mac OSX
Programming Language: C++, Java, SQL

Honor

Academic Excellence Scholarship   October 2017- Present

if it is above 3.0. List your degrees in reverse chronological order. Projects that hosted or participated can also be listed to show the unique ability.

4. Honor and Activities

In this section, honor such as fellowships and scholarship, major awards given by official groups, could be included. Activities, such as leadership in groups as well as experience in campus organizations, honor society and volunteer groups.

5. Working Experience

The information in Work Experience section includes position or job title, organization, duration of the employment, and other details such as job duties and special responsibilities. In addition, you need to summarize your achievements and skills from the experience, and use action verbs to describe your experience. In English version of your resume, use past tense verbs for jobs held in the past and present tense for job you still have.

When writing a resume, you need to first consider the background, construct the headings and arrange the facts into groups. In the whole content of the resume, you need to show more about how you can help the company rather than what an amazing person you are.

Furthermore, first impression is very

照时间倒叙列出。可以列上曾经主持或参与过的项目以显示独特性。

4. 荣誉与活动

荣誉包括奖学金、官方团体颁发的主要奖项等；活动包括官方或利益团体中的领导角色以及在校园组织、荣誉协会和志愿者团体中的经验。

5. 经验

工作经验包括岗位名称、组织、工作时间和其他与工作职责相关的信息。从经验中总结成就和技能，用动作动词来描述你的经验。英文版简历用过去时态动词来描述过去从事的工作，用现在时态来描述你仍然从事的工作。

写简历时，需要首先考虑背景，构建标题，并将内容分类。在简历中你需要展示如何能更好地帮助公司而非单纯展示自己有多么出色。

此外，第一印象非常重

important. Your resume needs to get employer's attention as quickly as possible. In resume scanning stage, a HR can decide whether to schedule an interview with a candidate within only a few minutes, even a few seconds. Therefore, bullet format is recommended to make reading easier. The candidate may list 3～8 statements and customize the quality to fit the job requirements.

13.4　Job Application Letter

1. The Purpose of Job Application Letter

A job application letter is a way to introduce you and your resume to your target employer. It is regarded as a cover letter of your resume. The purpose of a job application letter includes:

(1) describe your skills and experiences in words and highlight key messages;

(2) provide more information about your target position and reflect your competitive advantages;

(3) and show your writing skills and abilities through words.

2. Tips for Job Application Letter

The job application letter normally includes 4 parts: heading, opening, body and closing sections.
(1) Heading.

In order to make it easier to identify, you can use the same heading in your resume including your formal full name and contact information.

要。在简历筛选阶段，HR可以在几分钟甚至几秒钟就决定是否会邀请求职者参加面试。因此，为便于阅读，建议采用项目列表排版，总结出3～8条最符合工作邀请的特征。

四、求职信

1. 求职信的目的

求职信是向雇主介绍自己和简历的一种方式。求职信中你可以用文字重点描述能体现竞争优势的技能和经验，突出关键信息，并通过文字展示你的写作技巧和能力。

2. 书写建议

求职信通常包括四个部分：标题、开头、正文和结尾。
（1）抬头。

求职信可以使用与简历相同的抬头，包括姓名和联系信息，以便于识别。

The information of the recipient is also essential in the heading, which should include salutation, position title, company name and company address. Remember to address the letter to an individual by name. If you are not able to find a particular name or identify the contact, you may address the letter to the general position, for example, "Director of Human Resource". If you are sending it by email, the subject can be the application for a specific position "An Application for Business Analyst".

(2) Opening.

The opening is the first paragraph of a job application letter, which is usually three or four sentences long. In this paragraph, you should better mention where you got the recruiting information from. If you are recommended by a person, you may mention his or her name. State briefly why you are interested in the position and the organization. You may also summarize 2-3 of your best skills that make you fit the job and be more detail in the body. The most important thing is to be creative so as to get the reader's attention.

(3) Body.

The body of your job application letter should be one or two paragraphs, not being too long. In this part, you need to demonstrate how your background fill the requirements by outlining assets, special skills and soft skills you own that related to your target position. However, avoid repeat from the resume, just emphasize one or two quality or skills that can be your highlight.

收件人信息应包括称谓、职务等。求职信应有明确的收件人，若不清楚联系人姓名或无特定联系人，可将信件发给相关职务人员，例如人力资源总监。如果通过电子邮件发送，可以将拟申请的职位名称列在邮件主题中，例如"业务分析师申请"。

（2）开头。

开头不宜过长，需要包含应聘岗位、招聘信息获取渠道、应聘原因等内容。可以简要列举自己适合该岗位的简要原因，在正文中详细阐述。开头应有特色和创新，以吸引读者注意。

（3）正文。

求职信正文中需要展示自己与岗位匹配的原因并给予具有说服力的解释与信息，避免重复简历内容。

(4) Closing.

You can close your job application letter with "Sincerely" "Cordially" "Best Regards", etc.

Skip three to four spaces for your written signature and sign your name in the space. If you have attached your resume after your job application letter, type "Enclosure" to remind the reader or "Attached" if you are sending it by email.

（4）结尾。

应使用礼貌用语作为求职信的结尾。

正文与签名落款间应空三到四行。若随信附有简历，应注明"附件"以作提醒。

Tips on writing a job application letter:

Gain attention in the opening;

Select the content that requires further description in the letter;

Organize for conviction which the recruiters want. You need to put more emphasis on how you can help the company instead of what you can do;

Drive for action in the close, for example asking for an interview;

Customize job application letter for each target position;

Control the letter in one page;

Use the "You" view;

Use a traditional letter style;

Use no templates.

A Sample of Job Application Letter

December 16, 2018

Ada Smith

LTC Business Consulting

ABC Road, Room 306

New York City

Dear Ms. Ada:

At the career fair held by LTC, I am honored to have a chance meet with one of your human resource agents. We spoke about the position of Business Analyst in your New York Office. LTC Business Consulting has always been one of the top organizations in the consulting industry, known for professionalism and data analysis.

In my educational background in business science, I have taken course work in business data analysis, business management and database design. These courses provided me with the foundation for my devotion as a member of your company.

During my study at D University, I have had the opportunity to be involved in various organizations and groups which has allowed me to widen my view as well as get in touch of members from different majors and fields. The experience of the vice president of Financial Management Association teach me how to accommodate with others and how to make critical decisions in a large organization. During the 6 months internship in the National Bank, I took part in miscellaneous projects including loan proposals for customers, managed forecast reports and gross margin reports and assist data analyzing system with database tools like Microsoft Access. With the combination of financial knowledge and data analysis tools that meets your company's key business needs. I have been really interested in using data analyzing tools in solving financial related problems, and I think that really connects with LTC Business Consulting.

The resume has been enclosed. I can be reached at the number or email address stated above. Thank you for your time and consideration.

Regards,
Lucy White

Lucy White
Enclosure

【Conclusion】本章小结

A resume is a highly personalized and persuasive summary of a person's background, experience, education, and skill level that shows your qualifications for a job with a specific employer. The resume should involve name and contact information, capabilities and skills, education, achievement, working experience, other skills and activities.

According to format, there are 3 major types, which are chronological resume, functional resume and combination resume. A chronological resume is a resume format that displays work experience in chronological order. A functional resume is a resume that emphasizes the skills, abilities, qualifications, achievements, etc. of a job seeker but not related to a particular employer. The combination resume is a resume that combines a chronological resume with a functional resume.

Self-evaluation is the first step of producing a good resume. Before you start writing a resume, you need to first think about your strengths and weaknesses, interest, and skills. Personal branding not only involves the skills and work experience that is included in the resume, but also shows overall image, such as personality, social circle, resources, etc.

A job application letter is a way to introduce you and your resume to your target employer, which mainly including heading, opening, body and closing sections.

【Exercises】实务练习

Action verbs are critical in writing a resume. Please refer to the action verbs in Table 13.2, and complete the following exercises.

Exercise 1: Please write a resume by using appropriate action verbs.

Exercise 2: Please write a job application letter to introduce you and your resume to your target employer.

Table 13.2　Action Verbs in a Resume

Management Skills			
Administered	Analyzed	Assigned	Attained

(To be continued)

(Continue)

Management Skills			
Chaired	Consolidated	Contracted	Coordinated
Delegated	Developed	Directed	Enhanced
Established	Evaluated	Executed	Increased
Improved	Initiated	Instituted	Managed
Motivated	Organized	Oversaw	Planned
Prioritized	Produced	Recommended	Reorganized
Reviewed	Scheduled	Strengthened	Supervised
Marketing Skills			
Advocated	Broadcasted	Circulated	Created
Customized	Designed	Devised	Developed
Disseminated	Distributed	Endorsed	Formulated
Illustrated	Influenced	Informed	Marketed
Personalized	Presented	Promoted	Propagated
Publicized	Published	Represented	Sold
Sales Skills			
Assured	Clarified	Communicated	Compelled
Consulted	Converted	Convinced	Encouraged
Endorsed	Guided	Influenced	Inspired
Interpreted	Motivated	Negotiated	Personalized
Persuaded	Presented	Promoted	Prompted
Provoked	Recruited	Sold	Stimulated
Financial Skills			
Administered	Allocated	Analyzed	Appraised
Apportioned	Assessed	Audited	Balanced
Budgeted	Calculated	Compared	Computed

(To be continued)

(Continue)

Financial Skills			
Counted	Developed	Estimated	Evaluated
Forecasted	Formulated	Gauged	Managed
Marketed	Planned	Priced	Projected
Processed	Quantified	Reconciled	Reduced
Customer Service Skills			
Accommodated	Adjusted	Advised	Agreed
Arranged	Assisted	Assured	Consulted
Contributed	Cooperated	Counseled	Ensured
Facilitated	Guaranteed	Guided	Influenced
Mediated	Moderated	Modified	Motivated
Negotiated	Personalized	Persuaded	Provided
Reassured	Reconciled	Related	Requested
Resolved	Respected	Served	Sold
Clerical Skills			
Approved	Arranged	Catalogued	Charted
Classified	Coded	Collected	Compiled
Dispatched	Distributed	Executed	Generated
Implemented	Inspected	Maintained	Monitored
Operated	Organized	Prepared	Processed
Purchased	Recorded	Retrieved	Reviewed
Routed	Scheduled	Screened	Set up
Standardized	Systematized	Tabulated	Updated
Validated	Verified		
Leadership Skills			
Administered	Allocated	Appointed	Approved

(To be continued)

(Continue)

Leadership Skills			
Assigned	Authorized	Awarded	Conducted
Controlled	Delegated	Designed	Directed
Disapproved	Discharged	Encouraged	Enforced
Evaluated	Executed	Governed	Hired
Led	Managed	Oversaw	Presided
Recommended	Regulated	Required	Selected
Settled	Signed	Specified	Sponsored
Stipulated	Supervised		
Communication Skills			
Addressed	Advertised	Authored	Called
Circulated	Coached	Collaborated	Communicated
Composed	Conferred	Contacted	Convinced
Corresponded	Directed	Discussed	Drafted
Edited	Elicited	Emphasized	Explained
Formulated	Influenced	Informed	Instructed
Interpreted	Lectured	Mediated	Moderated
Negotiated	Oriented	Persuaded	Presented
Promoted	Publicized	Recommended	Reconciled
Recruited	Redirected	Referred	Related
Represented	Resolved	Showed	Spoke
Translated	Transmitted	Tutored	Wrote
Creative Skills			
Acted	Adapted	Authored	Composed
Conceptualized	Created	Conceived	Customized
Designed	Developed	Directed	Established

(To be continued)

(Continue)

Creative Skills			
Estimated	Fashioned	Forecasted	Formulated
Founded	Generated	Illustrated	Initiated
Instituted	Intergrated	Introduced	Invented
Investigated	Modified	Originated	Performed
Planned	Proposed	Researched	Revised
Revitalized	Set up	Shaped	Solved
Teaching Skills			
Adapted	Advised	Coached	Communicated
Coordinated	Developed	Enabled	Encouraged
Evaluated	Explained	Facilitated	Focused
Guided	Individualized	Informed	Instructed
Persuaded	Stimulated	Trained	Tutored

【Study Questions】课后问题

1. What sections should be included in a resume?
2. What contents should be included in a cover letter for job application?

Chapter 14   Business Writing

第14章   商务写作

In business, communication includes oral and writing. Any document used for business communication, such as email, letters, reports, and proposals, needs to be developed upon specific business writing norms.

Through this chapter, you will be able to:
- understand the general process of writing and learn basic writing tips;
- apply the skills to write proposals, reports and business email.

商务沟通包括口头和书面两种沟通形式。任何用于商业交流的文档,如电子邮件、信件、报告和建议书,都具有特定的商业写作规范。

通过本章的学习,你将能够了解写作的一般流程及写作建议;掌握书写常用企划、报告和商务邮件的技能。

14.1   The General Process of Business Writing

一、商务写作的基本流程

Business writing is different from ordinary information editing in terms of business communication norms. No matter writing a business report or a memo, you should set clear goals first. You may start by asking yourself the following questions: What's the purpose of this document? Who is the audience? Is this document urgent? How to avoid the risk of leaving a negative record by writing?

The process of business writing includes six steps: research, clustering, formatting, drafting, revising and proofreading.

商务写作在商务沟通规范方面不同于一般的信息编辑。无论是写商业报告还是备忘录,你都应该首先设定明确的目标。思考几个基本问题。

商务写作流程主要包括调研、组织、提炼、起草、修改、校对六个步骤。

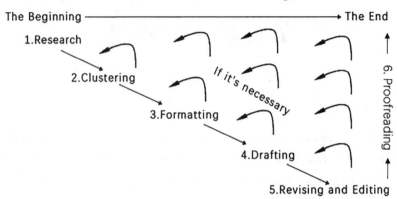

Figure 14.1 The Process of Writing
图 14.1 写作流程

1. Research

Adequate research is the basis of good business writing. Research refers to the stage of information and data searching. What should be included in the research usually depends on both the goal of the author and the reader. There are many ways to collect data, including primary data and secondary data. Primary data refers to the data obtained through the direct efforts of the researcher through surveys, interviews and direct observation. For example, opinions from stakeholders after the interview, notes taken in a meeting, results of brainstorming, etc. Secondary data refers to the data obtained through published sources, such as internal documents, Internet, database, financial statements, publications, video materials, survey reports, blogs, etc. It is also more current and more relevant to the research project.

1. 调研

充分调研是商务写作的基础。调研是指在写作前的资料调查阶段，调研的内容通常取决于文件的阅读者以及写作者的目标。调研资料可分为一手资料和二手资料。一手资料指写作者亲自调查所获得的资料，包括采访相关者后所得的意见、会议后的笔记、头脑风暴后的结果等；二手资料指他人发布的相关文件，如文档、互联网信息、数据库、财务报表、出版物、视频材料、调查报告、博客等。

2. Clustering

Clustering is a part of planning, while less structured than formatting. Clustering allows the author to gather abundant of ideas which are generated after research. The most common ways of clustering are grouping similar ideas together and composing a blueprint.

Grouping similar ideas together is a basic method for beginners. For example, the author can divide a series of action ideas into pre-event actions, in-event actions and post-event actions, put them into related groups and make sure that they are in the right place.

Mind mapping is a highly effective way of clustering information. All Mind Maps have some things in common. They have a natural organizational structure that radiates from the center and use lines, symbols, words, color and images according to simple, brain-friendly concepts. Mind mapping converts a long list of monotonous information into a colorful, memorable and highly organized diagram that works in line with your brain's natural way of doing things. In the structure of mind mapping, the main idea, subject or focus is crystallized in a central image; the main themes radiate from the central image as "branches", which form a connected nodal structure; topics of lesser importance are represented as "twigs" of the relevant branch.

When clustering, make sure the bases are covered by answering the questions of "Ws and

2. 组织

组织是形成提纲与写作计划的一部分，结构性较弱。最常见的方法是将类似内容归类，形成思维导图。

可将相似的想法进行分组。例如，将一系列的行动理念分为事前、事中和事后行动，将它们分为相关的组。

思维导图是一种组织信息的高效方法。构建自然的组织结构，从中心辐射，使用线、符号、文字、颜色和图像，思维导图将单调的信息转换成丰富多彩、高度组织化的图表，与大脑自然的思考方式一致。在思维导图的结构中，主要的思想、主题或焦点置于中心意象中；主要的主题以"分支"的形式从中心意象中辐射出来，形成一个相连的节点结构；次要的主题以相关分支的"分支"来表示。

Hs" including *Why, Who, What, When, Where, How, How Much and So What.*

Figure 14.2　Mind Map
图 14.2　思维导图

3. Formatting

Formatting is further thinking through a certain format based on the formation of basic arguments and ideas. The PAPER format and PRESS format are most commonly used formats in business writing.

PAPER refers to Purpose, Action, Particular, Evidence and Request for Response. The author needs to figure out why he/she is writing, what action he/she plans to adopt, whether the particular details are ready, whether there is enough material support, what the next step is. It can be seen as a process of giving out information about current situation and asking for a feedback.

PRESS refers to Point (or Problem), Reason,

3. 设计

设计是在论点和思想基础上，基于某种设计进行进一步思考。

PAPER格式包括目的、行动、特别事项、证据、回复请求等内容。

PRESS格式包括问题点、

Example or Evidence, Solution and benefits of solution and Supporting Material. The author needs to consider about the contents including what the subject is, what is the support statement, what are the remedies, solutions, suggestions, ideas and plans. It can be seen as a process of putting forward a plan over a particular problem.

Through formatting and the establishment of the framework, the author can ensure the logic order of the content, making it easy for readers to understand as well as achieving their own goals.

4. Drafting

In the process of drafting a document, freewriting is a practical strategy intended to encourage the development of ideas without concern for the conventional rules of writing.

Freewriting requires the author to write freely and quickly, which means to immediately write down what appears in mind based on the preliminary outline. The author should not care about the order of writing or edit while writing.

It has been proven that freewriting can help author express ideas more effectively and completely and provide the most complete material for later revising. When freewriting is initially adopted, the author will inevitably be affected by the framework. This step is to encourage the author to separate drafting from editing for efficient writing.

5. Revising and Editing

Revising and editing is an essential and

理由、例子或证据、解决方式及其收益、支持材料等内容。

通过格式化设计和建立框架，可确保逻辑顺序，使读者更容易理解，并实现写作目标。

4. 起草

在起草文件过程中，自由写作是一种实用的写作技巧。

自由写作要求作者在写作过程中自由快速地写作，这意味着要根据初步的大纲，立即写下作者脑海中出现的东西。事实证明，自由写作能够帮助作者更有效完整地表达其思路，为后期的修改与编辑提供最为完整的素材，更有利于完整表达和高效写作。

5. 修改

修改和编辑是一个必要

possibly repetitive procedure of writing. There are also differences between revising and editing. The former mainly is the adjustment of the overall content and style, while the latter includes the change of micro-problems such as words, punctuation and grammar. Business writing requires a combination of both parts to complete a good document.

When revising, the strategy and macroscopic changes should be made first. The author needs to consider:
(1) Whether the document achieve the communication goals with the target audience;
(2) Whether the document reads credible, culturally adapted and reasonable;
(3) Whether the language style is appropriate and meets expression requirements;
(4) Whether the current paragraph composition and order are the best;
(5) Whether some transition words and connectives are appropriate;
(6) Whether the language expression is accurate and clear;
(7) Whether it is easy to cause misunderstanding.

Editing needs to be carried out after revising is completed. It is important not to pay too much attention to wording in revising inorder to prevent you from losing the trees for the forest. When editing, the author needs to:
(1) Use more main important sentence in a paragraph;
(2) Avoid too long words and sentences;
(3) Edit the wrong grammar, punctuation, and

的，也可能是重复的写作过程。修改和编辑之间也存在差异。前者主要是对整体内容和风格的调整，后者则包括词类、标点、语法等微观问题的润色。商务写作需要两个部分的结合来完成一个好的文档。

在修改部分，首先要在策略和宏观上进行修改。作者需要考虑目标读者和沟通目标，可信度、文化适应性、合理性，语言风格，段落之间的连接性等。

编辑需要在大体修改完成之后进行，切忌在整体修改中过度关注措辞等问题，以避免顾此失彼。在编辑时，作者需要注重语句的简洁性、准确性与结构多样性以及单词的词性和态度。

spelling to ensure accuracy and clarity;
(4) Enhance the diversity of sentence patterns;
(5) Carefully use positive or negative words and usually show a more positive attitude;
(6) Use verbs, nouns and adverbs appropriately;
(7) Use parallel structure properly;
(8) Identify clear words and fuzzy words;
(9) Distinguish and identify words with similar but different meanings;
(10) Use simple sentences;
(11) Reasonable use of comparison.

6. Self-Proofreading and Feedback from Others

After finishing the preliminary manuscript, another important process is proofreading. The author could do self-proofreading or asking for feedbacks from others. In managerial context, the feedbacks from team members are especially important.

In both ways of proofreading, the author or team members should:
(1) try to read the printed version ;
(2) read the meaning aloud ;
(3) read only one word at a time when checking spelling ;
(4) proofread the title and subtitle ;
(5) proofread the format and font.

When proofreading is completed, it is usually necessary to repeat the process of revising and editing.

6. 自我校对与他人反馈

初稿完成后要进行校对，作者可自己校对或寻求他人反馈。特别是来自团队成员的反馈意见尤为重要。

在校对的过程中需要注意尽量阅读打印版；大声读出意思；在检查拼写时一次只看一个词；记得校对标题和文题；记得校对文稿的格式和字体等。

校对完成后，通常需要进行一轮修改和编辑。

14.2 Proposals and Reports

1. Business Proposals

A business proposal is a document used to offer specific goods or services to potential customers at a defined cost. They are typically used by B2B companies to win new business and can be either solicited or unsolicited.

An excellent business proposal includes several key elements, including an executive summary, project details, timeline, terms, and cost, as well as a conclusion and signature field for the prospect. Completing a proposal requires the author to have a clear understanding of the problems to be solved, the investigations to be completed and the opportunities to be grasped.

The following are some tips on writing a business proposal:

(1) Problems or opportunities. In the background part, the author needs to define the problems to be solved and opportunities to arouse audience interests on the project.

(2) Reason. Assume the consequences to individual or organization if the problem is not solved or missed the opportunity. Put forward the necessary basic factors like money, time, personnel and social support.

(3) Solution. Provide an effective and feasible solution. To enhance credibility, the author should demonstrate the validity of your data and information sources, the feasibility of your proposal through deduction and propose the research topic.

二、商业计划书和报告

1. 商业计划书

商业计划书是用于向潜在客户以一定价格提供特定商品或服务的文件。可以是被征求或主动提出的。

一份优秀的计划书应包括执行摘要、项目详细信息、时间线、条款和成本，以及潜在客户的结论和签名字段。完成一个企划书需要写作者对自己要解决的问题，需要完成的调查与想要把握的机会有清晰的认识。

企划书写作时需要注意的要点，包括问题或机会、原因、解决方式、能力、时间、价格、最终产品等。

(4) Ability. Show that you or your organization has ability and resource including knowledge, channel, human resources, experience to carry out the solutions above to do the task. This can be demonstrated by current enterprise data and past successful cases.

(5) Time. Provide a detailed schedule of the project, which includes tasks, division of labor, deadline, etc.

(6) Price. Detailed budget is crucial for a business proposal, including cost on materials, salary, commission, service charge, and expenses on travel and other fees.

(7) The final product. Emphasize achievable goals, benefits and final products or service that you or your organization can offer.

When writing a proposal, you may make use of templates created by business experts. A request for proposal (RFP) is basically a publication of detailed requirements by a prospective buyer in order to receive vendor offerings. In order for the requester to evaluate and compare all offers in a fair, easier, and faster manner, this publication is usually a formal document advising and guiding the prospective contractor through the whole procurement process (solicitation, selection, and award). To do so, the RFP document describes all the information surrounding the project, among other things.

征求建议书是关于向外招标详细要求的一种基本的文件。为了以更公平、便捷及快速的方式对所有的竞标进行评估，该建议书常常是正式的文件，以建议并引导未来的合同方完成整个竞标过程（询价，选择，授权），建议书描述了项目相关的所有信息。

2. Reports

A report usually refers to a genre that provides information, data or suggestions for an organization, enterprise or individual to make

2. 报告

报告通常指可以为组织、企业或个人提供制定计划或解决问题信息、数据或建议

plans or solve problems. Based on contents, it can be divided into information reports, analytical reports and recommendation reports.

Information report refers to a report that only provides readers with a large amount of information and data without further conclusions.

Analysis report refers to the report that draws out conclusion after analysis based on the information and data provided by the information report, but such report will not give solutions or suggestions.

Recommendation report is the report that provide recommendations for operational solutions based on analysis.

The problems specified in the report need to be real, worthwhile, focused, and challenging. Among them, pertinence is a very important feature. The author must narrow down the topic at the beginning. For example, the report topic of improving team performance is too broad. Which team is the team need to be analyzed? How do you measure performance? Are there any specific indicators that can be used as targets? Is there a time limit for this task? How long does it take to finish the task? These problems can be identified at the beginning and then more operational conclusions and actions can be obtained. Therefore, it will be more practical if the topic is changed to "how to make the sales team achieve 1.5 to 2 times the sales results within 6 months?"

Information and data are the basis of reports.

的文体；根据内容可以分为信息报告、分析报告和建议报告。

信息报告提供大量信息和数据，但不给出深入结论。

分析报告在信息报告所给出的信息和数据的基础上进行分析后得到结论，但不会给出解决方案或建议。

建议报告则是在分析基础上提供推荐解决方案或建议的报告，具有操作性。

报告中规定的问题需要真实、有价值、聚焦并具有挑战性。其中，针对性是一个非常重要的要求。作者必须在开始时缩小主题范围。

举例来说，"关于提升团队绩效的报告"作为报告主题太宽泛了，应该聚焦到具体针对的团队，绩效的界定、时限等。"关于促进销售团队6个月内销售额提升1.5~2倍的报告"作为报告主题就更清晰了

信息和数据是报告的基

Investigation is a "must do" process in the writing of reports to obtain a certain amount of accurate and effective data and information. If you want to obtain data or information indirectly, the author can search the relevant information from the Internet or other channels. In fact, writing a high-quality report requires the author to obtain first-hand information and data. Interviews and questionnaires are the most commonly used methods. An interview is a structured conversation with someone who can give you useful information. Questionnaire can survey a group of people. The most common method is to design a questionnaire and ask the target group to fill in it so as to collect information.

14.3　How to Write a Business Email

Email is commonly used in business writing. The body of the email can be either a formal notification or a daily work memo, depending on the relationship between the author and the reader, the purpose, tone and style of the content.

Email is probably the most common format in business writing. In many cases, the email sender is not able to get expected feedbacks from the receiver. There could be many reasons, such as whether the contents of this e-mail is clear, the information is sufficient, the wording and way of expression is appropriate, or the request is explicit.

The basic parts that form a formal business email include the title, salutation, body, ending,

础。为了获得准确有效的数据和信息，需要进行必要的调查。间接数据或信息可以从互联网或书籍中搜索获取；采访、问卷调查是最为常用的获取第一手资料的方法。采访是与能够给你有用信息的人进行一个结构性的对话交流，记录相关信息和数据。问卷调查最常见的是设计问卷后让目标人群填写，进而收集信息。

三、商务电子邮件写作

邮件是商业沟通交流中最常用的一种文体，电子邮件的正文可以是正式通知，也可以是日常工作备忘录。

在很多时候，发件人无法从收件人处得到其想要的回复。原因通常在于邮件内容是否清晰，信息传递是否充足，措辞与执行方式是否恰当，要求是否明确。

邮件的构成包括主题、称呼、正文、结尾以及落款。

and signature.

1. Subject

The subject is the first impression an email makes. The subject answers the question "Why am I writing?" A good email title should give the recipient adequate accurate information and show professionalism.

1. 主题

主题是电子邮件给人的第一印象。主题回答了"为什么我要写这封邮件?"好的主题应给收件人足够的准确信息,并显示出专业性。

Tips on writing subject part of an email:
(1) Fill in the subject. The email without subject is very rude and unprofessional. The recipient even may not open the email.
(2) Maximize the use of the subject bar and try to put important information or information that describes the importance of the message in the subject bar, such as deadlines, reminders of importance, etc.
(3) Use colon and dash reasonably in the subject and use the logo to clear and simplify the theme, such as Mid-term Proposal — Reply by June. 24. Use semicolons and dashes reasonably in the subject.
(4) Reduce the number of words in the subject, such as thank you, hello, etc. It is easy to make the mail default to spam.

主题写作小贴士:务必不要空缺主题栏从而使邮件"无主题";最大化使用标题栏并提示重要信息;在主题中合理使用分号和破折号;减少以"感谢""您好"等作为主题。

2. Salutation

At the beginning of the mail, it is necessary to call the recipient politely. If the recipient is client or superior, the author can use the courtesy name of Sir. / Madam, Mr. /Mrs. / Miss, or the corresponding identity of the person followed by last name, such as Dear Mr. /Ms. (last name). For

2. 称呼

在邮件的开头,应礼貌地称呼收件人。如果收件人是客户或上级,作者一般应尊称收件人的姓氏加上相应职务身份,或姓名加上先生/女士/小姐等尊称;对于与同

internal mail communication with colleagues, the author can directly use first name, for example, Hi Ming (first name); Hello Mary (first name); Dear Shaoteng (first name).

3. Body

The body is the main part of an email. In most cases, the body of email is shorter than other business writing genre, putting more emphasis on efficiency and simplicity, so that the recipient can get the necessary information in a short period of time. Complex and important information exchange is usually completed by telephone, face-to-face communication, etc., while mail is mostly an auxiliary means.

Tips on writing body part of an email:
(1) The body needs to have a basic framework. You can take the PAPER or PRESS format above as a reference to express the your idea in a short article.
(2) The first sentence of the main content should be short, clear and powerful. The main purpose of greeting and expressing the mail is to let the reader grasp the key points at the beginning.
(3) Summarize the information at the beginning in the long e-mail. In the case of long email, it is necessary to sort out the logic of the article as a whole at the beginning, so that the reader can understand the content as the reader expected and review conveniently later.
(4) Chunk information into manageable parts. On the basis of information summary, the content of the mail can be divided into relative parts with the means of segmentation and subtitle. If the corresponding action is required, an action should be announced at the beginning or end of each part to ensure that the content is clear enough.
(5) Highlight important information instead of burying deep in paragraphs.

事的内部邮件通信，可以直接使用名字。

3. 正文

正文是电子邮件写作的主要部分。一般而言，电子邮件正文比其他商业写作体裁短，更强调效率和简明性，以便收件人迅速获得必要信息。复杂而重要的信息交流通常应通过电话、面对面交流等方式完成，而邮件仅作为辅助手段。

The important information in the paragraph can be emphasized by different colors, fluorescence, size, etc., which is easy for the reader to leave a deep memory. Be careful not to be too fancy, or it will cause reading difficulties.

(6) Use headings reasonably. The subtitle makes it easy for the author to summarize the contents of each paragraph, so that the structure is clear and the reader can remember the core content.

(7) Control the length of the sentence. The sentence should not too long, which is no more than 2.5 lines. Try to use short sentences. If the sentence is too long, it is easy to cause difficulties in reading.

(8) Use professional tone. Try to avoid the expression of spoken language and the use of words that are too emotional.

(9) Use verbs. The use of verbs can make the sentence simpler and more straightforward, and the emphasis on key information will be more obvious. For example, "We need to complete this paper by Thursday" instead of "The completion of this paper is Thursday."

(10) One screen. Long emails lead to an increase in reading difficulty, which may increase the possibility of communication errors.

正文写作小贴士：正文需要有基本框架，且首句简短、清晰和有力。长邮件在开头梳理线索分成可操作的部分，标出重点信息，使用标题，控制句子长度。在专业性方面注重语气与用词。

4. The Ending

Usually, an email is ended with greetings. Generally, in internal mail communication, "Thanks" and "Best regards" are more common.

4. 结尾

结尾处应合理使用问候语或祝语。

Depending on the formality, the writer can use:
常见英文邮件结尾用词
- Respectfully yours
- Kindest regards

- Very truly yours
- Yours truly
- Sincerely yours
- Cordially
- Regards
- Best regards
- Yours
- Thanks

5. Signature

A full signature has the following elements: name, position, department, company name, contact number including phone number, telephone number, fax number, email address, company website.

5. 落款

落款需要包括名字、职位、部门、公司名称、联系方式、公司网址等元素。

Example:
Anderson
Senior Manager
Marketing Department
IRT Co., Ltd
Phone: 63485295
Tel: 14739523093
Fax: 33335125
Email: anderson@irt.cn
Web: www.irt.com

Avoid tables or graphics in the signature. This will eat up storage capacity and don't always translate to readers outside your organization.

If you include signature for each email, your reader won't have to scan the email trail for you contact information. At minimum, give your telephone number.

落款应避免用图片形式，以免占用存储空间或在发送中读取失败。

6. Special Sending Tools

In some special occasions, some convenient tools can be used as appropriate when sending email.

(1) Reply all.

Replying all means replying the message to the sender and all recipients. If everyone belongs to the same team and the communication is frequent, using reply all will be the fastest way to share information. However, the use of Reply All is more of risk and may lead to leakage of information. Overuse may result in the flood of mail. Remember a rule: Use this function only if you are sure that everyone in the sender and recipient list need this information.

(2) Forwarding message.

Forwarding message refers to sending a received email to an individual or multiple people, which is a commonly used function in daily email communication. If you forward message to more than one person at a time, you need to record the recipients to avoid the situation of forwarding to the same person multiple times, which may cause information confusion. The reason and situation of forwarding should be explained in the body of the forwarded mail. Most importantly, don't forward some confidential emails to others without the original author's consent.

(3) CC

CC, known as carbon copy, means that coping a message to the person related and the recipients can see each other. If you use CC,

6. 特殊发件方式

发送电子邮件时可以根据需要使用一些方便的工具。

（1）回复全部。

回复全部是指将邮件回复至发件人和所有收件人。只有在你确定发件人和收件人列表里的所有人都需要这一信息时再使用这一功能。

（2）转发。

转发是指将收到的邮件发送给相应的个人或多人，是日常邮件沟通中较为常用的一个功能。如一次转发多人，应避免多次转发，造成信息混乱。同时在转发的邮件正文中说明转发的原因和情况。最重要的是，不要未经原作者同意就将一些机密邮件转发给其他人。

（3）抄送。

抄送，指将一封邮件抄送给与邮件相关的人，收件人相互之间可以互相看见。

pay attention to avoid overly specific names and content in the body of the email. Remember that this email is sent to a large audience. Be clear about who needs this information and avoid receiving information such as "Why send this email to me". When replying to a CC message, do not reply all the recipients of the CC email, which can be embarrassing.

(4) BCC.

BCC stands for blind carbon copy. The recipients in the BCC field receives the e-mail but unbeknownst to those in the TO and CC fields. The BCC feature provides a variety of possibilities for mail usage. Using BCC in multi-directional communication makes it easy for the recipient to reply directly to you, avoiding the situation of replying to all recipients. If you add yourself to the recipient of the BCC, you can effectively archive the messages you have sent.

如选择了抄送，注意邮件正文中避免出现过于针对性的称呼和内容。当回复一个抄送邮件时，避免将抄送的所有收件人都作为回复对象，否则容易造成尴尬的情况。

（4）密送。

密送是在抄送邮件的基础上，收件人无法看到其他收件人。在同时多向沟通中使用密送可以方便收件人直接对你进行回复，避免出现回复所有收件人的情况。将自己加入密送的收件人可以将所发送的邮件存档。

【Conclusion】本章小结

The formal writing process mainly involves six steps including researching, clustering, formatting, drafting, revising, and proofreading. PAPER format and PRESS format are most commonly used formats in business writing.

In this chapter, we introduced some basic genres of business writing, which are business proposals, reports, and emails. The readers need to pay attention to the important elements in email writing, and practice on writing a formal business email.

【Exercises】实务练习

How to Write a Business Email?

According to the main content, business email can be divided into request emails, follow-up emails and reminder emails.

1. Request Email

Request email is a message asking the receiver to do something. When writing a request business email, the author needs to:

(1) Focus on the information you need immediately. Put forward your call for action at or near the opening of the email.

(2) Tell the receiver why you need the information or you want to make this move.

(3) Emphasize the due date of your call and put the due date in a paragraph in a special paragraph if it is very important or urgent. To seem polite, the author can use phrase like "at your earliest convenience" or "as soon as possible".

(4) Offer further information, contacts, phone numbers or essential materials for the receiver to make quick and useful response easily.

Example:

Dear Chris,

　　Thank you for your preparation and time on this project.

　　I have attached the process charts you requested.

　　As to the exact due date, Jenny will coordinate with the supervisors involved and let you know by July 14th.

　　Since this construction addition plan is not in our original approved budget, I would appreciate it if you could provide me with some cost information.

　　Thank you very much.

　　Best regards,

　　Tom

2. Follow-up Email

Follow-up email is the email that follows up to the original messages and requests that has been sent before. In the content of the email, the author can:

(1) State immediately that the email is a follow-up and restate your original messages and requests.

(2) Offer an excuse for the receiver's previous failure to reply in time. The excuse should be one that will allow him/her to save face for not responding

or acknowledging the message.

(3) Emphasize the critical need for a response. If you can, find reader incentive for the action. If appropriate, state your next action if you get no response to make your point.

Example:

Dear Jeffery,

　　As a follow-up to our phone conversation last week, I wanted to get back to you about the budget plan of Orders X35 we have discussed.

　　I can understand how busy you are this time of year, especially with budget reviews going on. However, I would really appreciate it if you could update me on the status of this order by Thursday so that I can inform our customer.

　　I hope we can have a reply from you by May 26th so we can promote the next step of sales.

Sincerely Yours,
Jane

---

3. Reminder Email

The reminder email is the kind of email whose main content is what you wish to remind the receiver about and his/her expected action. In reminder email writing, the author should:

(1) Make the reminder as complete as the first announcement. Repeat all necessary information — time, date, place, purpose, topics of concern, deadlines, and so forth.

(2) Mention the word "reminder" in both the subject line and the body of the mail.

(3) Call special attention to the changes from the former plan or announcement. Place that detail alone in a separate paragraph or underline or capitalize it to add emphasis.

(4) Request confirmation at the end if needed.

Example:

Dear Stella,

  Recognizing your busy schedule, I'm just writing to remind you of the upcoming sales management seminar on March 25th. You were recommended by your chief sales manager to represent the sales representatives in your team. Please check your name and contact information in the attached Excel file of the seminar attendees.

  If at all possible, would you please reply to this email if you plan to attend by this Friday? In this way we can distribute training materials in advance.

  I'm sincerely looking forward to hearing from you.

Best regards,
Timmy

Exercise:

(1) Write an email to your subordinate — the sales representative, to request for the latest monthly sales report.

(2) Email your business partners to politely ask them to follow-up the documents for next round of negotiation.

(3) Write a reminder email to your boss to request feedbacks on your report.

【Study Questions】课后问题

1. What are the six steps involved in the formal writing process?
2. What are the basic parts in an email?
3. How to write the subject of an email?

References

参考文献

［1］James S. O'Rourke. 管理沟通［M］. 康青译. 中国人民大学出版社，2015.
［2］Kitty O.Locker. 商务与管理沟通（原书第10版）［M］. 张华等译. 机械工业出版社，2013.
［3］克里斯·安德森. 演讲的力量：如何让公众表达变成影响力［M］. 蒋贤萍译. 中信出版集团股份有限公司，2016.
［4］安德鲁·索贝尔，杰罗德·帕纳斯. 提问的艺术：为什么你该这样问［M］. 陈艳译. 中国人民大学出版社，2013.
［5］哈特斯利，麦克詹妮特. 管理沟通原理与实践（英文版·原书第3版）［M］. 葛志宏，孙卉译. 机械工业出版社，2008.
［6］Hodgetts, Richard M. Cross-cultural Communication and Management［M］. 人民邮电出版社，2008.
［7］魏江等. 管理沟通：成功管理的基石（第4版）［M］. 机械工业出版社，2019.
［8］康青. 管理沟通（第5版）［M］. 中国人民大学出版社，2018.
［9］张莉. 管理沟通（第2版）［M］. 高等教育出版社，2011.
［10］张振刚，李云健. 管理沟通：理念、方法与技能［M］. 机械工业出版社，2014.
［11］李映霞. 管理沟通：理论、案例与实训［M］. 人民邮电出版社，2017.
［12］赵洱紫. 管理沟通：原理、策略及应用［M］. 高等教育出版社，2017.

图书在版编目(CIP)数据

管理沟通:原理与实践:英、汉/张琰主编. —上海:复旦大学出版社,2020.9
(复旦卓越.21世纪管理学系列)
21ISBN 978-7-309-15338-5

Ⅰ.①管… Ⅱ.①张… Ⅲ.①管理学-高等学校-教材-英、汉 Ⅳ.①C93

中国版本图书馆 CIP 数据核字(2020)第 170127 号

管理沟通:原理与实践(双语)
张　琰　主编
责任编辑/王雅楠

复旦大学出版社有限公司出版发行
上海市国权路 579 号　邮编:200433
网址:fupnet@fudanpress.com　　http://www.fudanpress.com
门市零售:86-21-65102580　　团体订购:86-21-65104505
外埠邮购:86-21-65642846　　出版部电话:86-21-65642845
常熟市华顺印刷有限公司

开本 787×960　1/16　印张 14.5　字数 260 千
2020 年 9 月第 1 版第 1 次印刷

ISBN 978-7-309-15338-5/C·403
定价:40.00 元

如有印装质量问题,请向复旦大学出版社有限公司出版部调换。
版权所有　　侵权必究